Diet recommendations for chronic renal insufficiency

Please check these recommendations always with a nutrition consultant, therapist, doctor or dietician. The recipes and the list of ingredients are supporting the conventional medical therapy.
The calorie disclosures of fresh ingredients (fruit and vegetables) vary according to quality and time of harvest. The contents were checked by a dietician and a nutrition consultant for the Traditional Chinese Medicine (TCM).

AF198747

Author:
©2019 Josef Miligui
www.ebns.at

Source:
The lists are created from the EBNS database for nutritional counseling. The database is used by dietitians, therapists and doctors for advising the patient / client.

Literature:
The specialist literature and the training documents of the German and Austrian dietary and traditional Chinese medicine serve as a knowledge base. We have used the documents as a basis of knowledge, adapted it to our experience and completed them.
http://di-book.com

Production and publishing:
BoD – Books on Demand, Norderstedt
ISBN: 9783746025698

Diet recommendations for DIETETICS - Protein and electrolyte - kidney - chronic renal insufficiency

1   Treatment strategy 4
2   Avoid... 4
3   Breakfast 4
4   Snack.. 5
5   Lunch.. 5
6   Afternoon 6
7   Dinner 6
8   Any time.. 7
9   Recipes... 8
   9.1   Antipasti... 8
   9.2   Apple and celery soup with roasted fennel 9
   9.3   Apricot and cranberry ice cream 10
   9.4   Asparagus Cream Soup... 10
   9.5   Avocado with lemon 11
   9.6   Baked chicory 12
   9.7   Basic recipe for a reissue soup (Congee) 12
   9.8   Basic recipe for a vegetable soup, nutritious 13
   9.9   Basmati rice + Zucchini tofu dish 14
   9.10   Boiled celery salad with exotic spices 14
   9.11   Carrot and potato rucola sandwich........................... 15
   9.12   Carrot and rice gruel soup 16
   9.13   Carrot drink... 16
   9.14   Carrot Risotto.. 17
   9.15   Celery and potato cream soup 18
   9.16   Champignon rice 18
   9.17   Champignon salad with cress..................................... 19
   9.18   Chicory salad with tangerine 20
   9.19   Cold cherry soup with curd cheese dumpling.......... 21
   9.20   Cucumber salad 22
   9.21   Cucumber soup 22
   9.22   Fennel-Rice Soup.. 23
   9.23   Frozen pineapple juice 23
   9.24   Fruit juice 23
   9.25   Grapefruit juice 24
   9.26   Grated apple.. 24
   9.27   Hearty polenta mash 25
   9.28   Kohlrabi in chervil sauce with potatoes 25
   9.29   Lasagne with tofu cream 26

9.30	Lentil and chestnut soup with curry	27
9.31	Oat Congee	28
9.32	Oatmeal soup with spring onion and carrots	28
9.33	Paprika-tomato rice	29
9.34	Pear juice	29
9.35	Polenta with peach	30
9.36	Potato gnocchi with vegetables and basil sauce	30
9.37	Potato with dandelion salad	32
9.38	Pumpkin soup	32
9.39	Radish with sugar	33
9.40	Refreshing cucumber soup with potatoes	33
9.41	Rice congee with carrots and fennel	34
9.42	Rice congee with chicken liver and buckthorn fruit	35
9.43	Rice with parsnips	35
9.44	Rice with stewed vegetables	36
9.45	Roasted millet with plum compote	37
9.46	Rosemary Potatoes	37
9.47	Semolina soup with vegetables	38
9.48	Spicy Tofu Vegetable Pan	38
9.49	Spring salad	39
9.50	Thick pea soup	40
9.51	Vegetable miso soup with tofu	41
9.52	Vegetable rice	41
9.53	Vegetable semolina soup	42
9.54	Warming carrot soup	43
9.55	Wheat semolina with olives-herb-sauce and salad	44
9.56	Zucchini semolina cream soup	45
10	Effects of food	46
10.1	Use ingredients: recommendable	46
10.2	Use ingredients: yes	46
10.3	Use ingredients: little	49
10.4	Do not use contra-acting foods	53
11	Complementary	53
11.1	Bath for purification	53
11.2	Birch leaves	54
11.3	Cress	54
12	Basics of Nutrition	55
12.1	Nutrition	55
12.2	Recipes	57
12.3	Foodstuffs	57
12.4	Herbs	58
13	Other dietic-books	59
14	EBNS - Software for nutritional counseling	61

1 Treatment strategy

Protein standardized diet (0.8 g per kg) with particular reference to the biological value and sufficient energy supply;
Prefer drinks and food with little sodium, phosphates and potassium.

2 Avoid

Sodium-, potassium- and phosphorus-rich food and drinks.
Biologically low quality protein.

3 Breakfast

kkal. per serving

Apricot and cranberry ice cream 106
Avocado with lemon 289
Baked chicory 230
Boiled celery salad with exotic spices 165
Carrot and potato rucola sandwich 94
Carrot and rice gruel soup 101
Carrot drink 143
Carrot Risotto 308
Champignon rice 410
Cucumber soup 95
Fennel-Rice Soup 155
Fruit juice 175
Grated apple 120
Hearty polenta mash 262
Kohlrabi in chervil sauce with potatoes 187
Oat Congee 162
Oatmeal soup with spring onion and carrots 134
Pear juice 180
Polenta with peach 197
Potato with dandelion salad 162
Radish with sugar 46
Refreshing cucumber soup with potatoes 148
Rice congee with carrots and fennel 131
Rice with parsnips 206
Roasted millet with plum compote 139
Semolina soup with vegetables 105

Spicy Tofu Vegetable Pan 241
Thick pea soup 123
Vegetable miso soup with tofu....................................... 106
Vegetable rice... 303
Vegetable semolina soup 198
Wheat semolina with olives-herb-sauce and salad 244

4 Snack

Carrot and potato rucola sandwich.................................... 94

5 Lunch

Antipasti 100
Apricot and cranberry ice cream...................................... 106
Asparagus Cream Soup 240
Avocado with lemon.. 289
Baked chicory 230
Basmati rice + Zucchini tofu dish.................................... 145
Boiled celery salad with exotic spices 165
Carrot and potato rucola sandwich.................................... 94
Carrot and rice gruel soup 101
Carrot drink..... 143
Carrot Risotto.. 308
Celery and potato cream soup 112
Champignon rice... 410
Champignon salad with cress.. 220
Chicory salad with tangerine 256
Cold cherry soup with curd cheese dumpling........................... 320
Cucumber salad.. 27
Cucumber soup 95
Fennel-Rice Soup 155
Frozen pineapple juice.. 29
Fruit juice 175
Grated apple 120
Hearty polenta mash... 262
Kohlrabi in chervil sauce with potatoes 187
Lasagne with tofu cream.. 301
Lentil and chestnut soup with curry 175
Oat Congee 162
Oatmeal soup with spring onion and carrots 134
Paprika-tomato rice... 291
Pear juice.. 180
Polenta with peach 197

Potato gnocchi with vegetables and basil sauce 166
Potato with dandelion salad 162
Pumpkin soup 104
Radish with sugar 46
Refreshing cucumber soup with potatoes 148
Rice congee with carrots and fennel 131
Rice congee with chicken liver and buckthorn fruit 175
Rice with parsnips 206
Rice with stewed vegetables 166
Roasted millet with plum compote 139
Rosemary Potatoes 188
Semolina soup with vegetables 105
Spicy Tofu Vegetable Pan 241
Spring salad 180
Thick pea soup 123
Vegetable miso soup with tofu 106
Vegetable rice 303
Vegetable semolina soup 198
Warming carrot soup 133
Wheat semolina with olives-herb-sauce and salad 244
Zucchini semolina cream soup 146

6   Afternoon

Carrot and potato rucola sandwich 94

7   Dinner

Apricot and cranberry ice cream 106
Asparagus Cream Soup 240
Avocado with lemon 289
Baked chicory 230
Boiled celery salad with exotic spices 165
Carrot drink 143
Carrot Risotto 308
Celery and potato cream soup 112
Champignon salad with cress 220
Cold cherry soup with curd cheese dumpling 320
Fennel-Rice Soup 155
Frozen pineapple juice 29
Fruit juice 175
Grated apple 120
Hearty polenta mash 262
Kohlrabi in chervil sauce with potatoes 187

Lasagne with tofu cream 301
Lentil and chestnut soup with curry 175
Oat Congee 162
Paprika-tomato rice 291
Pear juice 180
Polenta with peach 197
Potato gnocchi with vegetables and basil sauce 166
Potato with dandelion salad 162
Pumpkin soup 104
Radish with sugar 46
Refreshing cucumber soup with potatoes 148
Rice congee with chicken liver and buckthorn fruit 175
Rice with parsnips 206
Rice with stewed vegetables 166
Roasted millet with plum compote 139
Rosemary Potatoes 188
Semolina soup with vegetables 105
Spicy Tofu Vegetable Pan 241
Vegetable miso soup with tofu 106
Vegetable semolina soup 198
Warming carrot soup 133
Wheat semolina with olives-herb-sauce and salad 244

8   Any time

Apricot and cranberry ice cream 106
Avocado with lemon 289
Basic recipe for a reissue soup (Congee) 140
Carrot and rice gruel soup 101
Carrot drink 143
Frozen pineapple juice 29
Fruit juice 175
Grated apple 120
Oat Congee 162
Pear juice 180
Potato with dandelion salad 162
Radish with sugar 46
Rice congee with carrots and fennel 131
Rice with parsnips 206
Roasted millet with plum compote 139
Semolina soup with vegetables 105

9 Recipes

(rec.) = You can use more.
(little) = You should use less than specified
(no) omit.

9.1 Antipasti

Improves blood circulation, anti-inflammatory, relieves pain. Diuretic, promotes digestion, reduces blood pressure. antioxidative, antibacterial, affects anorexia, improves digestion, flatulence, stomach weakness, stimulating.
Cooking time approx. 40 min
3 portions to 246,67g. / 100kcal. - (carb:54% / prot:46%)
100g.=40,54kcal. / protein 2,74g. fat:5,6g.
µg. - Ph:7,93 Na:1,08 Ka:67,54 Mg:5,14 Ca:7,21 Fe:0,24 Zn:0,03 Col.:0 Hsr.:5,8

Quantity of ingredients:
Pepperoni 1 piece / 5g. (yes)
Lemon juice 1 table spoon / 10g. (yes)
Aubergine 1 piece / 300g. (yes)
Tomato 4 pieces / 200g. (yes)
Zucchini 5/8 oz / 200g. (yes)
Lemon peel 1/2 piece / 3g. (yes)
Olive oil 1 table spoon / 15g. (yes)
Basil (fresh) 8 leaves / 5g. (yes)
Salt 1 pinch / 0,5g. (little)
Coriander 1/2 teaspoon / 2g. (yes)

Cooking instructions:
Preheat the oven to 250 degrees Celsius and bake the hot peppers until the bowl becomes dark (about 20 minutes). Cover the hot peppers with a clear film and allow to cool. Peel the skin and cut into strips about 2 cm wide. Cut tomatoes in half and spread with oil in slices of aubergine and bake in the oven at 200 degrees golden brown (about 10 minutes) Fry the zucchini slices in the grill pan (without fat).
Mix everything together, mix the marinade of olive oil, salt and lemon peel and pour over the vegetables, sprinkle with coriander. Leave for 1 hour.

9.2   Apple and celery soup with roasted fennel

Reduces blood pressure, strengthens immune system, strengthens stomach, triggers stagnation, mineral and vitamin rich. Relieves constipation. metabolism-promoting and dehydrating healing effect.
Cooking time approx. 1 hour
Allergens: L
5 portions to 299g. / 191kcal. - (carb:65% / prot:35%)
100g.=63,75kcal. / protein 9,91g. fat:8,32g.
µg. - Ph:12,47 Na:9,59 Ka:40,8 Mg:12,03 Ca:47,53 Fe:0,26 Zn:0,01 Col.:0 Hsr.:6,06

Quantity of ingredients:
Celery root 1 piece / 350g. (yes)
Apple (sour) 1 piece / 175g. (little)
Onion white 1 piece / 100g. (yes)
Rapeseed oil 2 table spoons / 20g. (yes)
Basic recipe for a vegetable soup (nutritious) 2 1/4 cups / 600g. (little)
Fennel 1 piece / 150g. (yes)
Salt 1 pinch / 0,5g. (little)
Pepper (ground) 1 pinch / 0,1g. ()
1/2 cup / 100g. (little)

Cooking instructions:
Peel onion and celery and dice roughly. Peel the apple, quarter, remove the core, cut the apple into cubes.
Heat half of the oil in a large saucepan and fry the onion cubes in a medium heat for 2-3 minutes.
Add pieces of celery and pieces of apple and simmer for 1 minute. Add the vegetable broth according to the basic recipe, boil everything and cook over a low heat for about 45 minutes.
In the meantime, clean the fennel, wash and drain. Finely chop the fennel.
Heat a pan, add remaining oil and roast the fennel cubes in medium heat, stirring constantly, until well browned and tender. Season with salt and pepper and keep warm. Puree the soup ingredients in the broth with a hand blender. Brush apple celery soup through a sieve and pour it back into the pot. Add soy cream and heat everything again for about 1 minute. Season the apple and celery soup with salt and pepper.
Spread in the soup plate and serve garnished with the roasted fennel.

9.3 Apricot and cranberry ice cream

Forces resistance to infections, good to fight oral mucosal inflammation, diarrhea. Has a positive effect on the urinary tract.

Cooking time approx. 5 min

2 portions to 222,5g. / 106kcal. - (carb:91% / prot:9%)
100g.=47,87kcal. / protein 1,9g. fat:0,48g.
µg. - Ph:7,98 Na:0,94 Ka:107,17 Mg:4,69 Ca:8,02 Fe:0,03 Zn:0 Col.:0 Hsr.:8,57

Quantity of ingredients:

Apricots 3/4 lbs / 350g. (little)
Water 1/4 cup / 50g. (yes)
Cranberry 3 table spoons / 45g. (little)

Cooking instructions:

Mix the apricot juice with the cranberry syrup. Fill the juice into little molds, place in the freezer and let it freeze in about 3 hours.

9.4 Asparagus Cream Soup

Diuretic, improves blood circulation, prevents cancer, laxative, antiparasitic, stimulates liver function, good to fight loss of appetite, flatulence, rheumatism, heartburn.

Cooking time approx. 45 min

Allergens: ACG

2 portions to 409,5g. / 240kcal. - (carb:21% / prot:79%)
100g.=58,61kcal. / protein 5,2g. fat:19,85g.
µg. - Ph:9,44 Na:1,5 Ka:15,8 Mg:1,6 Ca:6,23 Fe:0,13 Zn:0,08 Col.:9,84 Hsr.:2,42

Quantity of ingredients:

Asparagus (green or white) 5/8 oz / 200g. (yes)
Water 2 cup / 500g. (yes)
Rapeseed oil 3 table spoons / 30g. (yes)
Wheat flour 2 table spoons / 10g. (yes)
Chicken yolk 1 piece / 25g. (yes)
Cow's milk (whole milk 3.5% fat) 1 table spoon / 15g. (little)
Sour cream 15% fat 1 table spoon / 15g. (little)
Pepper (ground) 1 pinch / 0,5g. ()
Nutmeg 1 pinch / 0,5g. (yes)
Lemon juice 1 teaspoon / 2g. (yes)
Parsley 2 table spoons / 20g. (yes)
Salt 1 pinch / 1g. (little)

Cooking instructions:
Wash and peel the asparagus.
Heat water, a little lemon juice and pinch of salt till it boils. Tie the asparagus spears together.
Add the asparagus peel to the cooking water and bring to the boil.
Add the asparagus and cook on low heat for about 20 minutes.
Then remove the asparagus bunches and pour the broth through a sieve.
For the roux, heat the oil in a saucepan, add the flour and sauté until it is colorless, slowly top up with the asparagus sauce and simmer for 10 minutes. Cut the asparagus spears into pieces about 3 cm long and place them to the soup.

Just before serving, bring the soup to the boil again.
Mix the egg yolk with the milk and sour cream.
Remove the pot from the heat and stir in the egg yolk and milk mixture.
Season with pepper and nutmeg, decorate with the chopped parsley and serve immediately.

9.5 Avocado with lemon

Good to fight insomnia, inflammation, swelling, pain and itching. Is calming.
Cooking time approx. 5 min
Allergens: 1 portion to 131g. / 289kcal. - (carb:17% / prot:83%)
100g.=220,61kcal. / protein 2,34g. fat:28,24g.
µg. - Ph:37,02 Na:5,86 Ka:469,27 Mg:29,31 Ca:11,83 Fe:0,59 Zn:0,37
Col.:0 Hsr.:29,01

Quantity of ingredients:
Avocado 1/2 piece / 120g. (yes)
Lemon juice 1/2 piece / 10g. (yes)
Salt 1 pinch / 1g. (little)

Cooking instructions:
Halve the avocado, remove the core, add the lemon juice, salt a little and eat with a spoon.

9.6 Baked chicory

Mineral supporter and is full of A-B-C vitamins.
Cooking time approx. 20 min
Allergens: AG
2 portions to 460,5g. / 230kcal. - (carb:74% / prot:26%)
100g.=50,05kcal. / protein 6,05g. fat:7,04g.
µg. - Ph:10,03 Na:4,19 Ka:30,57 Mg:4,66 Ca:5,41 Fe:0,15 Zn:0,07 Col.:0 Hsr.:4,48

Quantity of ingredients:

Chicory 4 pieces / 500g. (yes)
Cream, sweet 30% 2 table spoons / 40g. (little)
Breadcrumbs (wheat bread, bread roll) 2 table spoons / 20g. (yes)
Rice Basmati 1/2 cup / 60g. (yes)
Water 3 cups / 300g. (yes)
Salt 1 pinch / 1g. (little)

Cooking instructions:

Blanch chicory in hot water whole for about 5 minutes; place in a
casserole dish; put some sweet cream over it; put the bread crumbs
over the chicory and gratinate.
Place the rice in salted water, heat till it boils and let it simmer over low
heat for about 15 minutes.

9.7 Basic recipe for a reissue soup (Congee)

Low fat content, for the drainage of the body overweight and high blood
pressure.
Cooking time approx. 2-4 hours
3 portions to 273,33g. / 140kcal. - (carb:90% / prot:10%)
100g.=51,34kcal. / protein 2,96g. fat:0,48g.
µg. - Ph:1,95 Na:0,19 Ka:1,67 Mg:1,14 Ca:0,57 Fe:0,01 Zn:0,02 Col.:0 Hsr.:2,11

Quantity of ingredients:

Rice variety any 1 cup / 120g. (yes)
Water 6 cups / 700g. (yes)

Cooking instructions:

Cook rice and water in a ratio of about 1: 6. The amount of water
determines the thickness of the mash (matter of taste).
Put the rice in a saucepan with a heavy lid. It is important to simmer the
rice after a short boil on the slightest flame, otherwise it burns.
Boil the rice for 2-4 hours. The longer he cooks, the more he
strengthens.
If you want to eat the dish for breakfast, you can put the rice on just

before bedtime.
To be on the safe side, you should first check the behavior of your pot and cooker under observation for a similar amount of time, so that nothing burns. Refrigerate for later use.

9.8   Basic recipe for a vegetable soup, nutritious

Reduces blood pressure, strengthens immune system, prevents cancer, forcing spleen, dissolves stagnation, promotes weight loss. Good to fight immunodeficiency, high blood pressure, depressions, diabetes, diarrhea, reduces blood lipids.
Cooking time approx. 2-3 hours
Allergens: L
5 portions to 240,6g. / 48kcal. - (carb:71% / prot:29%)
100g.=19,87kcal. / protein 1,56g. fat:1,31g.
µg. - Ph:0,97 Na:0,73 Ka:5,14 Mg:0,36 Ca:1,26 Fe:0,02 Zn:0,01 Col.:0 Hsr.:0,56

Quantity of ingredients:
Olive oil 1 table spoon / 4g. (yes)
Onion white 1 piece / 60g. (yes)
Carrot 3 pieces / 200g. (yes)
Parsnip 3/8 lbs - 6oz / 150g. (yes)
Celery root 1 cup / 100g. (yes)
Ginger fresh 1/2 teaspoon / 2g. (yes)
Lemon 1/2 piece / 25g. (yes)
Juniper berry 6 pieces / 6g. (yes)
Thyme dried 1 pinch / 1g. (yes)
Lovage 1 table spoon / 3g. (yes)
Bay leaf 2 leaves / 1g. (yes)
Salt 1 pinch / 1g. (little)
Water 3 cups / 650g. (yes)

Cooking instructions:
Cut the vegetables into cubes.
Heat oil in hot pot, fry shortly onions and vegetables.
Add cold water, then add ginger, bay leaf and lemon juice.
Season with juniper, thyme and lovage. Cover for 2 - 3 hours on a low heat and simmer.
The used vegetables should be thrown away.
The basic recipe serves as a soup base and to refine vegetables, legumes or cereals.
If you want to eat vegetable soup immediately, add the desired vegetables half an hour before. Refrigerate for later use.

9.9 Basmati rice + Zucchini tofu dish

Diuretic, supports urination, harmonizes spleen and stomach, reduces flatulence, good to fight body overweight and high blood pressure.
Antioxidative, promotes digestion, perspiration, reduces blood lipids, forcing spleen.
Cooking time approx. 20 min
Allergens: E
4 portions to 306,75g. / 146kcal. - (carb:57% / prot:43%)
100g.=47,51kcal. / protein 7,95g. fat:4,89g.
µg. - Ph:13,21 Na:0,7 Ka:33,77 Mg:10,99 Ca:11,98 Fe:0,34 Zn:0,02 Col.:0 Hsr.:7,75

Quantity of ingredients:
Soy Tofu 5/8 lbs - 8oz / 250g. (little)
Olive oil 2 table spoons / 6g. (yes)
Coriander 1/2 teaspoon / 4g. (yes)
Ginger fresh 1/2 teaspoon / 4g. (yes)
Rice Basmati 1/2 cup / 60g. (yes)
Water 3 cups / 200g. (yes)
Zucchini 1 piece / 700g. (yes)

Cooking instructions:
Cut tofu cubes and marinate with olive oil, tamari, crushed coriander and ginger. Leave at least 1 hour.

Cook Basmati rice with the water. You can season with onion and cardamom.
Roast zucchini and tofu in pan in the hot oil for approx. 5-7 min.
Serve rice and tofu on a plate.
Add the parsley.

Can also be used as a salad for the home and on the go.

9.10 Boiled celery salad with exotic spices

Forcing spleen, relieves diarrhea, antibacterial, blood-forming, blood detoxifying, reduces inflammation, diuretic,
improves blood circulation.
Cooking time approx. 30 min
Allergens: GLMNO
4 portions to 341g. / 166kcal. - (carb:48% / prot:52%)
100g.=48,61kcal. / protein 5,59g. fat:9,17g.
µg. - Ph:3,39 Na:6,17 Ka:17,47 Mg:0,76 Ca:5,05 Fe:0,03 Zn:0,01 Col.:0,2 Hsr.:3,02

Quantity of ingredients:
Celery root 1 1/2 piece / 900g. (yes)
Yogurt (natural, 3.5% fat) 1 cup / 250g. (yes)
Sour cream 15% fat 2 table spoons / 20g. (little)
Turmeric (yellow root) 1 pinch / 1g. (little)
Sesame oil 1 table spoon / 20g. (little)
Pepper (ground) 1 pinch / 0,5g. ()
Onion white 1/2 piece / 25g. (yes)
Black caraway 1 pinch / 1g. (yes)
Salt 1 pinch / 1g. (little)
Lemon juice 1 piece / 40g. (yes)
Apple (sour) 1/2 piece / 100g. (little)
Vinegar (Apple vinegar) 1 dash / 3g. (yes)

Cooking instructions:
Cook the peeled celeriac in thick slices and then cut into bite-sized
strips.

Dressing: Mix a little yoghurt, sour cream, turmeric, sesame oil, pepper,
lemongrass powder, finely chopped onion, a little mustard, salt, crushed
black cumin, some cold water, lemon juice or vinegar; add the sour
chopped apple, some rose paprika, the lukewarm celery and mix well;
let it rest for 2 - 3 hours or overnight. Ideal as a substitute for raw food

9.11 Carrot and potato rucola sandwich

Reduces inflammation, improves digestion, supports urination, lowers
cholesterol, strengthens immune system, prevents cancer, good to fight
constipation (Fibre-rich), dissolves stagnation.
Cooking time approx. 20 min
Allergens: AG
4 portions to 116,25g. / 94kcal. - (carb:55% / prot:45%)
100g.=80,86kcal. / protein 2,68g. fat:2,83g.
µg. - Ph:4,15 Na:4,56 Ka:16,7 Mg:1,23 Ca:1,78 Fe:0,06 Zn:0,03 Col.:0,25 Hsr.:1,27

Quantity of ingredients:
Potato (mealy) 5/8 oz / 200g. (little)
Carrot 1 piece / 50g. (yes)
Sour cream 15% fat 3 table spoons / 45g. (little)
Onion (spring onion) 1 piece / 20g. (yes)
Rucola 1/2 bunch / 100g. ()
Lemon peel 1/4 teaspoon / 1g. (yes)
Salt 1 pinch / 1g. (little)
Pepper (ground) 1 pinch / 0,2g. ()

Cooking instructions:
Cook the potatoes gently, peel and squeeze through the potato press.
Cook vegetable broth according to the basic recipe and remove a carrot
after a short cooking time and finely crush
with a fork.
Stir the potatoes, carrots, grated lemon zest and sour cream into a
smooth cream.
Mix carrot and potato cream with finely chopped rocket salad. Season
the spread with salt and pepper and spread the bread. Sprinkle with the
finely chopped young onions.

9.12 Carrot and rice gruel soup

Stops diarrhea, good to fight fever, strengthens immune system,
reduces blood pressure.
Cooking time approx. 10 min
1 portion to 224g. / 101kcal. - (carb:96% / prot:4%)
100g.=45,09kcal. / protein 2,37g. fat:0,4g.
µg. - Ph:27,48 Na:20,34 Ka:65,63 Mg:170,89 Ca:178,57 Fe:1,03 Zn:0,34 Col.:0 Hsr.:12,3

Quantity of ingredients:
Basic recipe for a rice soup (Congee) 1 cup / 120g. (little)
Carrot 2 pieces / 100g. (yes)
Salt 1 teaspoon / 4g. (little)

Cooking instructions:
Peel and grate carrots. Heat the rice soup (according to the basic
recipe) till it boils and add the grated carrots and salt. Cook for 10
minutes.

9.13 Carrot drink

Promotes spleen and liver, reduces blood pressure, strengthens
immune system, prevents cancer, reduces radiation damage, diuretic,
building up, eye-enhancing, detoxifying, nerve-strengthening.
Cooking time approx. 15 min
Allergens: H
1 portion to 265g. / 143kcal. - (carb:81% / prot:19%)
100g.=53,96kcal. / protein 3,78g. fat:2,5g.
µg. - Ph:43,4 Na:22,3 Ka:117,79 Mg:18,2 Ca:36,26 Fe:1,83 Zn:0,55 Col.:0 Hsr.:17,98

Quantity of ingredients:
Millet flakes 1 table spoon / 10g. (yes)
Carrot 7/8 lbs / 200g. (yes)
Almond puree 1 teaspoon / 3g. ()
Honey 1/2 teaspoon / 2g. (yes)
Water 1/4 cup / 50g. (yes)

Cooking instructions:
Sprinkle millet flakes with 50 ml of cold water and let it swell for 10 minutes.
Juice the fresh carrots or use 200 ml. carrot juice.
Puree the millet flakes, carrot juice, almond paste and honey with the blender.

9.14 Carrot Risotto

Strengthens immune system, prevents cancer, loss of appetite, flatulence, high blood pressure, depressions, diabetes, diarrhea, stimulates liver function, dissolves stagnation.
Cooking time approx. 45 min
Allergens: GL
2 portions to 340,5g. / 308kcal. - (carb:84% / prot:16%)
100g.=90,46kcal. / protein 8,49g. fat:5,98g.
µg. - Ph:13,57 Na:9,57 Ka:29,14 Mg:16,17 Ca:58,13 Fe:0,33 Zn:0,11 Col.:0,3 Hsr.:7,34

Quantity of ingredients:
Olive oil 1/2 teaspoon / 5g. (yes)
Onion (spring onion) 2 table spoons / 7g. (yes)
Nutmeg 1 pinch / 0,3g. (yes)
Parsley 1/2 bunch / 25g. (yes)
Rice variety any 1/4 lbs - 4oz / 100g. (yes)
Carrot 5/8 lbs - 8oz / 250g. (yes)
Basic recipe for a vegetable soup (nutritious) 1 cup / 280g. (little)
Basil (fresh) 1/2 teaspoon / 2g. (yes)
Salt 1 pinch / 1g. (little)
Pepper (ground) 1 pinch / 0,3g. ()

Cooking instructions:
Heat the oil in a pan, fry the onions in a glassy and very soft manner. Add parsley, sauté briefly. Add rice, carrots and nutmeg, sauté briefly while stirring. Add the vegetable stock, season with fennel and basil, heat till it boils and cook for about 20 minutes until the rice and carrots are well. Stir from time to time and add some vegetable stock if necessary. The risotto should be slightly soupy. Just before the end of

the cooking time mix in the white wine and simmer the risotto for a short while. Remove risotto from the heat, mix in Parmesan.

9.15 Celery and potato cream soup

Reduces blood pressure, strengthens immune system, promotes weight loss. Good to fight immunodeficiency, loss of appetite, flatulence, depressions, diabetes, diarrhea, improves digestion.
Cooking time approx. 45 min
Allergens: GL
4 portions to 241,5g. / 113kcal. - (carb:83% / prot:17%)
100g.=46,69kcal. / protein 2,15g. fat:5,52g.
µg. - Ph:5,96 Na:3,46 Ka:23,98 Mg:22,27 Ca:83,51 Fe:0,18 Zn:0,01 Col.:0 Hsr.:1,49

Quantity of ingredients:
Olive oil 1 table spoon / 10g. (yes)
Onion white 1/2 piece / 25g. (yes)
Basic recipe for a vegetable soup (nutritious) 3 cups / 700g. (little)
Potato 5/8 oz / 200g. (little)
Nutmeg 1 pinch / 0,5g. (yes)
Ground 1 pinch / 0,5g. (yes)
Lemon peel 1/4 piece / 1g. (yes)
Crème fraiche cheese 2 table spoons / 20g. (little)
Salt 1 pinch / 1g. (little)
Parsley 1 table spoon / 8g. (yes)

Cooking instructions:
Heat the olive oil in a saucepan lightly. Fry the onions very gently in a mild heat. Pour with vegetable stock according to the basic recipe. Cover and cook for 15 minutes.
Add curd-cut potato, celery, nutmeg, cumin and lemon zest. Spice with salt and cook for 12 minutes. Potatoes and celery should be soft. Remove the lemon peel.
Puree the soup with crème fraiche using a blender. Season the soup with salt.
Arrange the soup in portions with the chopped parsley.

9.16 Champignon rice

Strengthens kidney, diuretic, warming the body from the inside, expands blood vessels, strengthens the muscles, promotes digestion and is good to fight high blood pressure, dissolves stagnation, promotes weight loss. Good to fight immunodeficiency, loss of appetite.

Cooking time approx. 30 min
Allergens: L
2 portions to 341g. / 410kcal. - (carb:89% / prot:11%)
100g.=120,23kcal. / protein 10,01g. fat:3,44g.
µg. - Ph:30,31 Na:3,54 Ka:32,26 Mg:27,24 Ca:62,74 Fe:0,37 Zn:0,16 Col.:0 Hsr.:12,22

Quantity of ingredients:
Onion white 1 piece / 50g. (yes)
Bay leaf 2 pieces / 1g. (yes)
Clove 2 pieces / 1g. (yes)
Basic recipe for a vegetable soup (nutritious) 7/8 lbs / 350g. (little)
Rice (whole grain) 5/8 oz / 200g. (yes)
Champignon 1/8 lbs - 2oz / 60g. (little)
Parsley 1/2 oz / 20g. (yes)
Pepper (ground) 1 pinch / 0,2g. ()

Cooking instructions:
Plug in the cloves in the onion. Heat the vegetable stock with the onion and the bay leaves till it boils. Add the rice to the boiling liquid, reduce the temperature to the lowest level and stir with the lid closed for 20-25 minutes.
In the meantime, wash the mushrooms, clean them, slice them, sauté briefly with a little water or sauté. Wash the parsley and chop finely.
Remove the onion from the rice, add the mushrooms and the parsley, season with pepper.

9.17 Champignon salad with cress

Promotes digestion and is good to fight high blood pressure. Good to fight loss of appetite, improves blood circulation.
Cooking time approx. 5 min
Allergens: AN
1 portion to 312g. / 220kcal. - (carb:56% / prot:44%)
100g.=70,51kcal. / protein 9,74g. fat:7,08g.
µg. - Ph:105,24 Na:37,35 Ka:366,67 Mg:14,25 Ca:19,03 Fe:1,08 Zn:0,41 Col.:0,02 Hsr.:60,22

Quantity of ingredients:
Champignon 5/8 lbs - 8oz / 250g. (little)
Sesame oil 2 table spoons / 6g. (little)
Pepper (ground) 1 pinch / 0,5g. ()
Salt 1 pinch / 1g. (little)
Lemon 1/2 piece / 15g. (yes)
Cress 2 table spoons / 10g. (yes)
White bread (wheat bread) 2 slices / 30g. (yes)

Cooking instructions:
Cut mushrooms into thin slices.
Dressing: sesame oil, a little ground pepper, salt, plenty of lemon juice, stir well the rose pepper; give over the finely chopped mushrooms; plenty of watercress.
Goes well with: white bread, round grain rice or quinoa; Along with the cereal, the salad makes a simple, light meal.
Serve with white bread.

9.18 Chicory salad with tangerine

Dissolves mucus, is rich in A-B-C Vitamins, promotes digestion, forcing spleen, promotes weight loss. Good to fight loss of appetite, flatulence, immunodeficiency.
Cooking time approx. 10 min
Allergens: AGNO
3 portions to 285g. / 257kcal. - (carb:75% / prot:25%)
100g.=90,06kcal. / protein 5,49g. fat:7,73g.
µg. - Ph:2,87 Na:5,09 Ka:18,76 Mg:1,33 Ca:3,14 Fe:0,04 Zn:0,01 Col.:0 Hsr.:2,36

Quantity of ingredients:
Tangerine 4 pieces / 300g. (little)
Chicory 2-3 pieces / 300g. (yes)
Sesame oil 2 table spoons / 18g. (little)
Pepper (ground) 1 pinch / 0,5g. ()
Salt 1 pinch / 1g. (little)
Vinegar Aceto Balsamico 2 teaspoons / 6g. (yes)
Lemon 1/2 piece / 25g. (yes)
Orange 1/2 piece / 70g. (little)
Orange jam 1 teaspoon / 4g. (little)
Cream, sweet 30% 1 table spoon / 10g. (little)
White bread (wheat bread) 6 slices / 120g. (yes)

Cooking instructions:
Peel tangerines and cut into bite-sized pieces; Cut chicory roughly and mix well.
Dressing: sesame oil, pepper, salt, raspberry vinegar or balsamic vinegar, a little lemon or orange juice, rose paprika, orange marmalade or, alternatively, another jam, stir well. Give a little sweet cream over the salad and let it
pass briefly.

9.19 Cold cherry soup with curd cheese dumpling

Improves blood circulation, reduces inflammation, good to fight
weakness, belching, diabetes, acute or chronic obstruction of the bowel.
Laxative, stimulates digestion, cleans the intestinal flora.
Cooking time approx. 2 hours and more
Allergens: GO
2 portions to 307g. / 320kcal. - (carb:70% / prot:30%)
100g.=104,23kcal. / protein 7,97g. fat:15,18g.
µg. - Ph:12,34 Na:3,16 Ka:31,13 Mg:2,66 Ca:11,16 Fe:0,08 Zn:0,05 Col.:1,51 Hsr.:2,44

Quantity of ingredients:
Cherry compote 7/8 lbs / 450g. (little)
Agar agar (kelp) 1/2 teaspoon / 1,5g. (yes)
Curd cheese 20% 1/4 lbs - 4oz / 100g. (little)
Sour cream 15% fat 1/8 lbs - 2oz / 50g. (little)
Vanilla sugar natural 1 package / 1g. (yes)
Sugar brown 1 table spoon / 10g. (yes)
Cinnamon ground 1 pinch / 0,5g. (little)
Lemon peel 1 pinch / 1g. (yes)

Cooking instructions:
Strain the cherry compote.
Finely puree half of the cherries with the cherry juice using a blender
and pass through a sieve.
Stir agar agar powder with cold water until smooth.
Bring the cherry puree to boil while stirring.
Mix in the agar-agar and cook the cherry puree for 1 minute while
stirring.
Spread hot cherry puree on two soup plates.
Sprinkle the remaining cherries into the soup.
Cool down cherry soup for 2 hours until lightly gelled.
Use the hand mixer to stir the cord cheese, sour cream, sugar, vanilla
sugar, cinnamon and lemon zest into a smooth, firm cream.
From the cream with the tablespoon, prick small dumplings and put
them into the cherry soup.

9.20 Cucumber salad

Diuretic, detoxifying, suppresses conversion of sugar into fat, lowers cholesterol, prevents cancer. Cucumber cools and moistens. Dill works against flatulence, anticonvulsant in gastrointestinal discomfort.
Cooking time approx. 5 min
Allergens: O
2 portions to 206g. / 27kcal. - (carb:68% / prot:32%)
100g.=13,11kcal. / protein 1,61g. fat:0,4g.
µg. - Ph:5,92 Na:2,32 Ka:35,15 Mg:2,16 Ca:4,03 Fe:0,12 Zn:0,05 Col.:0 Hsr.:1,94

Quantity of ingredients:
Cucumber 1 piece / 400g. (yes)
Salt 1 pinch / 1g. (little)
Dill 1 pinch / 1g. (yes)
Vinegar (Apple vinegar) 1 table spoon / 10g. (yes)

Cooking instructions:
Cut the cucumber (do not peel the BIO) thinly and season.

9.21 Cucumber soup

Diuretic, detoxifying, suppresses conversion of sugar into fat, lowers cholesterol, prevents cancer, promotes digestion, diaphoretic, dries out, good to fight yeast infections.
Cooking time approx. 20 min
Allergens: M
4 portions to 235,25g. / 96kcal. - (carb:22% / prot:78%)
100g.=40,6kcal. / protein 0,91g. fat:9,03g.
µg. - Ph:2,67 Na:1,28 Ka:15,6 Mg:1,17 Ca:2,57 Fe:0,06 Zn:0,01 Col.:0 Hsr.:0,85

Quantity of ingredients:
Olive oil 2 table spoons / 35g. (yes)
Cucumber 2 pieces / 400g. (yes)
Water 2 cup / 500g. (yes)
Sage 3 leaves / 3g. (yes)
Coriander 1 pinch / 1g. (yes)
Cardamom 1 pinch / 1g. (little)
Salt 1 pinch / 1g. (little)

Cooking instructions:
Heat oil and roast short the small cucumbers. Add Mustard seeds, coriander, cardamom and salt. Add water. Simmer for 10-15 min. Puree and decorate with fresh chopped sage.

9.22 Fennel-Rice Soup

Forcing spleen, relieves constipation, stimulates nerves, detoxifying, reduces inflammation, improves blood circulation.
Cooking time approx. 15-20 min
Allergens: EG
2 portions to 234g. / 156kcal. - (carb:88% / prot:12%)
100g.=66,45kcal. / protein 3,57g. fat:6,64g.
µg. - Ph:7,34 Na:16,24 Ka:41,07 Mg:52,9 Ca:55,34 Fe:0,27 Zn:0,06 Col.:1,92 Hsr.:2,45

Quantity of ingredients:
Basic recipe for a rice soup (Congee) 1 cup / 300g. (little)
Fennel 1/2 piece / 150g. (yes)
Butter organic 1 table spoon / 15g. (yes)
Soy sauce 1 dash / 3g. (little)

Cooking instructions:
Cook the fennel softly in the rice soup according to the basic recipe.
Before serving, add a piece of butter and some soy sauce.

9.23 Frozen pineapple juice

Pineapple reduce inflammation, supports urination, cleans the skin.
Cooking time approx. 1 1/2 hours
1 portion to 50g. / 29kcal. - (carb:95% / prot:5%)
100g.=58kcal. / protein 0,25g. fat:0,1g.
µg. - Ph:9 Na:2 Ka:173 Mg:17 Ca:16 Fe:0,4 Zn:0,3 Col.:0 Hsr.:7

Quantity of ingredients:
Pineapple 1/8 lbs - 2oz / 50g. (little)

Cooking instructions:
Juice pineapple yourself or freeze the organic pineapple juice in small portions and if necessary suck.

9.24 Fruit juice

Stops diarrhea, promotes digestion, appetizing, harmonizes the stomach, relieves pain, detoxifying, reduces blood pressure, strengthens immune system, prevents cancer, reduces radiation damage.
Cooking time approx. 10 min
2 portions to 305g. / 176kcal. - (carb:93% / prot:7%)
100g.=57,54kcal. / protein 1,89g. fat:0,9g.
µg. - Ph:4,99 Na:2,24 Ka:37,45 Mg:2,36 Ca:6,04 Fe:0,21 Zn:0,05 Col.:0 Hsr.:4,3

Quantity of ingredients:
Orange 2 pieces / 150g. (little)
Apple (sweet) 4 pieces / 300g. (little)
Carrot 2 pieces / 150g. (yes)
Honey 1 table spoon / 10g. (yes)

Cooking instructions:
Peel oranges and carrots. Cut all ingredients into cubes so that they fit into the juicer and juice. Sweet with honey.

9.25 Grapefruit juice

Promotes digestion, lowers blood glucose, dries out, provides Vitamin C
Cooking time approx. 5 min
1 portion to 250g. / 107kcal. - (carb:92% / prot:8%)
100g.=42,8kcal. / protein 1,5g. fat:0,5g.
µg. - Ph:17 Na:2 Ka:180 Mg:10 Ca:18 Fe:0,3 Zn:0,2 Col.:0 Hsr.:15

Quantity of ingredients:
Grapefruit (Pomelo) 1 cup / 250g. (yes)

Cooking instructions:
Juice fresh grapefruit or use organic juice.

9.26 Grated apple

Eat 3 times a day - Apple (sour) scraped and brown is stuffing. Relieves diarrhea.
Cooking time approx. 10 min
1 portion to 200g. / 120kcal. - (carb:94% / prot:6%)
100g.=60kcal. / protein 0,6g. fat:0,8g.
µg. - Ph:11 Na:3 Ka:144 Mg:6 Ca:7 Fe:0,5 Zn:0,1 Col.:0 Hsr.:15

Quantity of ingredients:
Apple (sour) 1 piece / 200g. (little)

Cooking instructions:
Peel apple and grate as fine as possible. Leave for at least 5 minutes until it turns brown.

9.27 Hearty polenta mash

Strengths spleen and stomach, promotes watering, promotes digestion, detoxifying, promotes perspiration, reduces blood lipids, stimulates, dissolves stagnation, stimulates appetite, dissolves stagnation.
Cooking time approx. 10 min
2 portions to 207,5g. / 262kcal. - (carb:80% / prot:20%)
100g.=126,27kcal. / protein 5,65g. fat:5,94g.
µg. - Ph:6,71 Na:0,73 Ka:11,2 Mg:2,2 Ca:2,17 Fe:0,09 Zn:0,05 Col.:0 Hsr.:2,46

Quantity of ingredients:
Corn Grease (Polenta) 1 cup / 120g. (yes)
Onion (spring onion) 2 pieces / 40g. (yes)
Ginger fresh 1/2 teaspoon / 2g. (yes)
Nutmeg 1 pinch / 1g. (yes)
Salt 1 pinch / 1c. (little)
Olive oil 1 table spoon / 10g. (yes)
Turmeric (yellow root) 1 pinch / 1g. (little)
Water 1 1/2 cups / 240g. (yes)

Cooking instructions:
Stir in the polenta in boiling water and let it swell for 7 min. Add green onion, grated ginger, turmeric, nutmeg, salt and olive oil and wait for 3 more minutes.

9.28 Kohlrabi in chervil sauce with potatoes

Reduces inflammation, lowers cholesterol, diuretic, conducts bowel winds, strengthens immune system, prevents cancer, promotes weight loss. Good to fight loss of appetite, flatulence, high blood pressure, depressions, diabetes, diarrhea.
Cooking time approx. 1 hour
Allergens: GL
4 portions to 316,75g. / 188kcal. - (carb:79% / prot:21%)
100g.=59,19kcal. / protein 8,66g. fat:2,51g.
µg. - Ph:2,95 Na:1,03 Ka:25,06 Mg:3,48 Ca:15,16 Fe:0,04 Zn:0,02 Col.:0,06 Hsr.:0,91

Quantity of ingredients:
Potato 6 pieces / 450g. (little)
Basic recipe for a vegetable soup (nutritious) 1 cup / 300g. (little)
Potato 1/4 lbs - 4oz / 100g. (little)
Nutmeg 1 pinch / 0,2g. (yes)
Lemon peel 1/2 teaspoon / 2g. (yes)
Ginger fresh 1/2 teaspoon / 2g. (yes)
Lovage 1/2 teaspoon / 2g. (yes)

Kohlrabi 3/4 lbs / 300g. (little)
Salt 1 pinch / 1g. (little)
Pepper (ground) 1 pinch / 0,2g. ()
Sour cream 15% fat 3 table spoons / 30g. (little)
Chervil dried 1 Bunch / 80g. (yes)

Cooking instructions:
Boil the potatoes in salted water.
Bring half of the vegetable stock to boil. Add the diced potatoes,
nutmeg, lemon zest, ginger and lovage. Cover the potatoes and cook
for about 10 minutes until soft and puree them with a blender until they
are smooth.
Bring remaining vegetable stock to boil. Cut kohlrabi into cubes and
add, cover and cook for about 8 minutes. Stir in the potato sauce and
heat everything briefly.
Puree with the mixing stick chervil and sour cream. Mix the chervil
cream with the kohlrabi vegetables.
Serve with the cooked, peeled potatoes.

9.29 Lasagne with tofu cream

Harmonizes spleen and stomach, reduces Flatulence, protects the
digestive system. Good to fight lack of appetite, flatulence, inflammatory
bowel disease, stomach ulcers, rheumatism, heartburn, twelffinger
intestinal ulcers.
Cooking time approx. 45 min
Allergens: ACEG
4 portions to 231g. / 301kcal. - (carb:50% / prot:50%)
100g.=130,3kcal. / protein 19,33g. fat:11,88g.
µg. - Ph:8,79 Na:3,51 Ka:7,05 Mg:4,06 Ca:7,27 Fe:0,09 Zn:0,05 Col.:3,83 Hsr.:3,82

Quantity of ingredients:
Soy Tofu 7/8 lbs / 400g. (little)
Chicken egg 2 pieces / 100g. (yes)
Onion white 2 pieces / 120g. (yes)
Tomato 1/4 lbs - 4oz / 100g. (yes)
Oregano dried 1 pinch / 1g. (yes)
Marjoram 1 pinch / 1g. (yes)
Salt 1 pinch / 1g. (little)
Noodles (wheat, lasagne) with egg 3/8 lbs - 6oz / 150g. (rec.)
Edam cheese 1/8 lbs - 2oz / 50g. (little)

Cooking instructions:
Tofu cream: Mix tofu with eggs, onions, small tomatoes, oregano, marjoram, peppers and some sea salt put into a smooth mass using a kitchen machine with a knife or a blender.

Lasagne: Place 1/5 of the tofu cream in a casserole dish (25x15cm), cover with 3 lasagna leaves, repeat this process twice, and then finish the last fifth of the tofu cream over the pastry plates. Sprinkle with a little grated Edam and bake in the oven at 175°C/347°F for about 1/2 hour.

9.30 Lentil and chestnut soup with curry

Reduces blood pressure, strengthens immune system, prevents cancer, reduces radiation damage, forcing spleen, dissolves stagnation, promotes weight loss. Good to fight immunodeficiency, loss of appetite, flatulence,
high blood pressure, depressions, diabetes, diarrhea.
Cooking time approx. 45 min
Allergens: LO
4 portions to 238,25g. / 175kcal. - (carb:83% / prot:17%)
100g.=73,45kcal. / protein 4,17g. fat:4,33g.
µg. - Ph:2,67 Na:3,8 Ka:7,98 Mg:4,63 Ca:15,86 Fe:0,06 Zn:0,02 Col.:0 Hsr.:2,07

Quantity of ingredients:
Lentils red 3/8 lbs - 6oz / 150g. (little)
Chestnuts 3/8 lbs - 6oz / 150g. (little)
Olive oil 1 table spoon / 10g. (yes)
Curry 2 teaspoons / 8g. (yes)
Basic recipe for a vegetable soup (nutritious) 2 cup / 500g. (little)
Turmeric (yellow root) 1 teaspoon / 2g. (little)
White wine 1/2 cup / 125g. (little)
Anise (Common Fennel) 1 pinch / 1g. (yes)
Cardamom 1 pinch / 0,5g. (little)
Parsley 2 table spoons / 6g. (yes)

Cooking instructions:
Add the olive oil to a pan, sauté the chestnuts, sprinkle with the curry, add the lentils and season with vegetable stock, add a little white wine, mix in the curcuma, simmer for about 20 minutes (until the chestnuts are tender).
Then puree the soup.
Taste with a pinch of anise, cardamom and herbal salt. At the end, sprinkle finely chopped parsley over it.

9.31 Oat Congee

Strengthens immune system.
Cooking time approx. 2-4 hours
Allergens: A
3 portions to 275g. / 162kcal. - (carb:74% / prot:26%)
100g.=58,91kcal. / protein 7,04g. fat:2,87g.
µg. - Ph:5,76 Na:0,23 Ka:5,98 Mg:2,27 Ca:1,82 Fe:0,1 Zn:0,08 Col.:0 Hsr.:2,51

Quantity of ingredients:
Oat 1 cup / 125g. (yes)
Water 6 cups / 700g. (yes)

Cooking instructions:
Cook oats and water in a ratio of about 1: 6. The amount of water determines the thickness of the mash (pure matter of taste). The oats swell, so do not take much. Put the oats in a saucepan with good insulation and a heavy lid. It is important to simmer the oats after a short boil on the slightest flame, otherwise it burns. Cook the oat for 2-4 hours. The longer it cooks, the more he strengthens.

9.32 Oatmeal soup with spring onion and carrots

Reduces blood pressure, strengthens immune system, prevents cancer, stimulates digestion, stimulates appetite, dissolves stagnation.
Cooking time approx. 30 min
Allergens: AG
3 portions to 266,33g. / 135kcal. - (carb:65% / prot:35%)
100g.=50,56kcal. / protein 3,87g. fat:5,59g.
µg. - Ph:3,67 Na:1,03 Ka:7,89 Mg:1,41 Ca:2,55 Fe:0,1 Zn:0,05 Col.:0,5 Hsr.:1,63

Quantity of ingredients:
Oat 6 table spoons / 48g. (yes)
Carrot 2 pieces / 200g. (yes)
Butter organic 1 table spoon / 15g. (yes)
Nutmeg 1 pinch / 1g. (yes)
Lovage 1 stem / 15g. (yes)
Onion (spring onion) 2 pieces / 40g. (yes)
Water 2 cup / 480g. (yes)

Cooking instructions:
Roast the oats in butter, add salt and spices, pour in water and heat till it boils. After 10 min. add the grated carrots and lovage, cook for 10 minutes. Finely add chopped onion.

9.33 Paprika-tomato rice

Good to fight little cholesterol, diabetes. Low in protein, low fat content, little protein. Forcing spleen, dissolves stagnation, promotes weight loss. Good to fight immunodeficiency, loss of appetite, flatulence, high blood pressure, depressions.

Cooking time approx. 25 min

Allergens: L

3 portions to 324g. / 291kcal. - (carb:89% / prot:11%)
100g.=89,92kcal. / protein 7,63g. fat:2,54g.
µg. - Ph:10,3 Na:1,31 Ka:15,5 Mg:9,5 Ca:22,5 Fe:0,14 Zn:0,06 Col.:0 Hsr.:4,12

Quantity of ingredients:
Onion white 1 piece / 50g. (yes)
Peppers 4 pieces / 120g. (yes)
Bay leaf 2 pieces / 1g. (yes)
Clove 2 pieces / 1g. (yes)
Basic recipe for a vegetable soup (nutritious) 7/8 lbs / 400g. (little)
Rice (whole grain) 5/8 oz / 200g. (yes)
Champignon 1/8 lbs - 2oz / 60g. (little)
Parsley 1/2 oz / 20g. (yes)
Peppers (rose peppers) 1 pinch / 0,2g. (yes)
Tomato 1/4 lbs - 4oz / 120g. (yes)

Cooking instructions:
Finely chop the onion. Cut the peppers into fine strips.
Heat margarine in a saucepan, sauté onions and peppers, and rice.
Add the vegetable stock, add cloves and bay leaves and leave to simmer in a closed pot for approx. 20 minutes. Cut the tomato meat into 1 cm cubes and add to the rice 5 minutes before the end of cooking.

9.34 Pear juice

Promotes digestion, supports urination.
Cooking time approx. 5 min

2 portions to 300g. / 180kcal. - (carb:93% / prot:7%)
100g.=60kcal. / protein 1,8g. fat:1,2g.
µg. - Ph:7,5 Na:1 Ka:62,5 Mg:3,5 Ca:4,5 Fe:0,15 Zn:0,05 Col.:0 Hsr.:7,5

Quantity of ingredients:
Pear 3 pieces / 600g. (little)

Cooking instructions:
Peel pears thinly (vitamins under the skin) and core. Juice in the juicer.

9.35 Polenta with peach

Relieves fatigue, forcing spleen, diuretic, strengthens the defense, good to fight fungi infections, lets urine and bile juice flow, prevents the aging process, strengthens brain cells.
Cooking time approx. 20 min
3 portions to 254g. / 197kcal. - (carb:89% / prot:11%)
100g.=77,56kcal. / protein 4,48g. fat:0,6g.
µg. - Ph:2,76 Na:0,12 Ka:11,83 Mg:0,93 Ca:1,02 Fe:0,05 Zn:0,02 Col.:0 Hsr.:1,56

Quantity of ingredients:
Water 1 1/2 cups / 240g. (yes)
Corn Grease (Polenta) 1 cup / 120g. (yes)
Peaches 2-3 pieces / 400g. (little)
Vanilla pod 1 pinch / 1g. (yes)
Chili (pod or ground) 1 pinch / 0,1g. (yes)
Cinnamon ground 1 pinch / 1g. (little)

Cooking instructions:
Pour the polenta into a pan of hot water with constant stirring until the polenta has the desired consistency. Pull the
polenta from the fire and let it soak for 10 minutes.

Wash fresh peaches and cut into quarters. Pour into the finished polenta the peaches, add the vanilla and add Chili
to taste, stir and let it go for 3 minutes.

Winter varieties: Pickled fruit, pear, apples

9.36 Potato gnocchi with vegetables and basil sauce

Strengthens immune system, promotes weight loss. Good to fight immunodeficiency, loss of appetite, flatulence, high blood pressure. Relaxing and reassuring.
Cooking time approx. 1 hour
Allergens: ACGL
4 portions to 290,25g. / 167kcal. - (carb:75% / prot:25%)
100g.=57,45kcal. / protein 6,54g. fat:4,63g.
µg. - Ph:3,26 Na:1,11 Ka:13,57 Mg:2,45 Ca:9,39 Fe:0,06 Zn:0,02 Col.:1,36 Hsr.:1,49

Quantity of ingredients:
Potato 5/8 lbs - 8oz / 250g. (little)
Wheat flour 1 oz / 25g. (yes)
Wheat semolina 1/2 oz / 15g. (yes)
Chicken yolk 1 piece / 20g. (yes)
Nutmeg 1 pinch / 0,2g. (yes)
Basic recipe for a vegetable soup (nutritious) 1 cup / 250g. (little)
Celery root 1/8 lbs - 2oz / 50g. (yes)
Lemon peel 1/2 teaspoon / 2g. (yes)
Ginger fresh 1/2 teaspoon / 2g. (yes)
Nutmeg 1 pinch / 0,2g. (yes)
Basil (fresh) 1 Bunch / 125g. (yes)
Crème fraiche cheese 1 table spoon / 20g. (little)
Salt 1 pinch / 1g. (little)
Pepper (ground) 1 pinch / 0,2g. ()
Carrot 1/4 lbs - 4oz / 100g. (yes)
Zucchini 1/4 lbs - 4oz / 100g. (yes)
Cauliflower 1/4 lbs - 4oz / 100g. (yes)
Broccoli 1/4 lbs - 4oz / 100g. (little)
Salt 1 pinch / 1g. (little)

Cooking instructions:
Steam the potatoes gently, peel and pass hot through the potato press.
Process the hot potatoes with flour, semolina, egg, nutmeg and salt to a
smooth dough. Let dough rest for 3o minutes.
Make small rolls (2 cm) out of the dough with flour-dusted hands, cut off
1 cm thin slices. To create the typical gnocchi shape, gently dab the
dough pieces with your thumb. Leave the gnocchi in lightly boiling
salted water for 6 - 8 minutes. Lift the gnocchi out of the pot with the
skimmer.

Heat the vegetable stock till it boils. Add diced celery, grated lemon
peel, finely chopped ginger and 1 pinch of nutmeg. Cover and simmer
for about 10 minutes. Using the blender, puree the vegetable broth,
celery, chopped basil and crème fraiche into a smooth sauce. Season
with salt and nutmeg.

Cut carrots, zucchini, cauliflower and broccoli into small pieces and
cook covered in a sieve over steam for 8 minutes until firm.
Heat the sauce again and add to the vegetables and arrange over the
gnocchi.

9.37 Potato with dandelion salad

Promotes spleen, reduces inflammation, improves digestion, regenerates skin, supports urinating, lowers cholesterol, detoxifying, reduces inflammation, forcing spleen and digestive system, detoxifying.
Cooking time approx. 25 min
2 portions to 203g. / 162kcal. - (carb:70% / prot:30%)
100g.=79,8kcal. / protein 4,28g. fat:5,59g.
µg. - Ph:26,58 Na:13,03 Ka:176,11 Mg:11,88 Ca:27,41 Fe:0,61 Zn:0,28 Col.:0,01 Hsr.:14,22

Quantity of ingredients:
Potato 5/8 lbs - 8oz / 250g. (little)
Onion white 1/2 piece / 20g. (yes)
Sunflower oil 1 table spoon / 10g. (little)
Dandelion (young plants) 1/4 lbs - 4oz / 125g. (yes)
Salt 1 pinch / 1g. (little)
Pepper white (ground) 1 pinch / 0,5g. (yes)

Cooking instructions:
Cook the potatoes in salted water and cut into thin slices. Finely chop the onion. Now season the potatoes with oil, salt and pepper and add the dandelion and mix.

9.38 Pumpkin soup

Promotes digestion, forcing spleen and stomach, reduces blood pressure, strengthens immune system, prevents cancer, reduces radiation damage, improves digestion, regenerates skin, lowers cholesterol, reduces blood glucose, protects liver.
Cooking time approx. 1 hour
3 portions to 236,33g. / 105kcal. - (carb:71% / prot:29%)
100g.=44,29kcal. / protein 2,54g. fat:3,64g.
µg. - Ph:4,02 Na:0,96 Ka:24,72 Mg:1,82 Ca:2,89 Fe:0,08 Zn:0,02 Col.:0 Hsr.:1,08

Quantity of ingredients:
Pumpkin 3/4 lbs / 300g. (yes)
Carrot 2 pieces / 100g. (yes)
Potato 2 pieces / 120g. (little)
Olive oil 1 table spoon / 10g. (yes)
Onion white 1 piece / 50g. (yes)
Water 1 cup / 120g. (yes)
Parsley 1 table spoon / 7g. (yes)
Anise (Common Fennel) 1 pinch / 1g. (yes)
Salt 1 pinch / 1g. (little)

Cooking instructions:
Add the olive oil to the pan, add the diced pumpkin, diced carrots and potatoes. Roast them shortly, add the finely chopped onion, fill with water, add enough water to cover the vegetables at least 3 finger-widths. Boil at low heat.

Season with sea salt, add small cutted parsley, a pinch of anise (little). Allow to simmer for about 35 minutes. Then purée the soup and add some water, depending on the consistency of the soup.

9.39 Radish with sugar

Promotes digestion, detoxifying, improves blood circulation, supports urination, reduces thirst, prevents cancer, strengthens body cells, dissolves stagnation, relieves weakness, promotes spleen, calms stomach, strengthens lung.
Cooking time approx. 5 min
2 portions to 202g. / 46kcal. - (carb:71% / prot:29%)
100g.=22,77kcal. / protein 2g. fat:0,4g.
µg. - Ph:7,18 Na:4,46 Ka:79,71 Mg:3,71 Ca:8,17 Fe:0,2 Zn:0,07 Col.:0 Hsr.:2,48

Quantity of ingredients:
Radish (white, green, purple-red) 1 piece / 400g. (yes)
Sugar brown 1 teaspoon / 4g. (yes)

Cooking instructions:
Grate the radish and sprinkle with sugar.

9.40 Refreshing cucumber soup with potatoes

Diuretic, detoxifying, suppresses conversion of sugar into fat, lowers cholesterol, prevents cancer, reduces inflammation, improves digestion, lowers cholesterol, dissolves stagnation, improves blood circulation, stimulates appetite.
Cooking time approx. 15 min
Allergens: GN
3 portions to 307,33g. / 148kcal. - (carb:70% / prot:30%)
100g.=48,26kcal. / protein 3,93g. fat:5,09g.
µg. - Ph:3,72 Na:0,77 Ka:23,54 Mg:1,43 Ca:2 Fe:0,05 Zn:0,02 Col.:0 Hsr.:1,19

Quantity of ingredients:
Sesame oil 1 table spoon / 10g. (little)
Potato 4 pieces / 300g. (little)
Onion (spring onion) 3 pieces / 60g. (yes)
Pepper (ground) 1 pinch / 0,5g. ()
Nutmeg 1 pinch / 1g. (yes)
Salt 1 pinch / 1g. (little)
Lemon 1/2 piece / 25g. (yes)
Cucumber 2 pieces / 500g. (yes)
Cream, sweet 30% 1 table spoon / 10g. (little)
Dill 1 table spoon / 15g. (yes)

Cooking instructions:
Sauté sesame oil, chopped potatoes, plenty of spring onions in a hot pot; add pepper, a little nutmeg, salt, lemon juice, hot water, diced cucumber; simmer for about 10 minutes and then puree; add some sweet cream as you like, and fresh dill.

Variation: Add a little chili, oregano, thyme or rosemary to soften the cooling effect.

9.41 Rice congee with carrots and fennel

Worms, forcing spleen, relieves constipation, stimulates nerves, detoxifying, reduces inflammation, improves blood circulation, reduces blood pressure, strengthens immune system, prevents cancer, reduces radiation damage.
Cooking time approx. 2 hours and more
Allergens: G
3 portions to 284,67g. / 131kcal. - (carb:94% / prot:6%)
100g.=46,14kcal. / protein 4,17g. fat:1,37g.
µg. - Ph:3,26 Na:3,23 Ka:18,37 Mg:21,62 Ca:22,98 Fe:0,13 Zn:0,03 Col.:0,09 Hsr.:1,26

Quantity of ingredients:
Basic recipe for a rice soup (Congee) 2 cup / 500g. (little)
Carrot 2 pieces / 100g. (yes)
Fennel 1 piece / 250g. (yes)
Butter organic 1 teaspoon / 3g. (yes)
Cardamom 1/2 teaspoon / 1g. (little)

Cooking instructions:
Cook rice congee according to basic recipe.
Clean and cut carrots and fennel.

When carrots and fennel are cooked from the beginning, they serve wholesomeness. If added shortly before the end of the cooking time, taste and vitamins are retained.

Refine with butter and cardamom before serving.

9.42 Rice congee with chicken liver and buckthorn fruit

Good to fight blood circulation disorders, thrombose, risk of embolism, high blood pressure, a headache, heart attack and stroke. Has many vitamins and minerals, high quality amino acid profile. Regulates the blood pressure and blood glucose level, forcing spleen.
Cooking time approx. 3 hours
Allergens: EO
3 portions to 307,67g. / 176kcal. - (carb:94% / prot:6%)
100g.=57,1kcal. / protein 7,51g. fat:1,45g.
µg. - Ph:4,49 Na:2,71 Ka:4,23 Mg:29,58 Ca:28,04 Fe:0,08 Zn:0,05 Col.:1,44 Hsr.:2,41

Quantity of ingredients:
Basic recipe for a rice soup (Congee) 5 cups / 800g. (little)
Chicken liver 1/2 cup / 60g. (little)
Bocksdorn fruits (Fructus Lycii, goji berry dried 1/2 cup / 60g. (little)
Soy sauce 1 dash / 3g. (little)

Cooking instructions:
Cook basic recipe for rice congee with the chicken liver and wolfberry fruits; Season with soy sauce.

9.43 Rice with parsnips

Rich in vitamins, minerals potassium and zinc. Good to fight blood circulation disorders, thrombose, risk of embolism, high blood pressure, a headache, heart attack and stroke, yeast infections.
Cooking time approx. 45 min
Allergens: 3 portions to 261,33g. / 206kcal. - (carb:78% / prot:22%)
100g.=78,95kcal. / protein 5,16g. fat:4,52g.
µg. - Ph:6,72 Na:0,7 Ka:31,66 Mg:2,54 Ca:3,53 Fe:0,05 Zn:0,07 Col.:0
Hsr.:4,06

Quantity of ingredients:
Rice variety any 1 cup / 120g. (yes)
Water 1 1/2 cups / 200g. (yes)
Salt 1 pinch / 1g. (little)
Parsnip 3-4 pieces / 450g. (yes)
Olive oil 1 table spoon / 10g. (yes)
Sage 1 teaspoon / 3g. (yes)

Cooking instructions:
Peel the parsnips and cut into slices. Fry for a short time in oil. Add the rice and fry again for a short time. Add the water and cook it at least 30 min. Sprinkle with fresh chopped sage.

9.44 Rice with stewed vegetables

Reduces blood pressure, strengthens immune system, prevents cancer, reduces radiation damage, extremely low fat content, good to fight blood circulation disorders, thrombose, risk of embolism, a headache, heart attack and stroke. Is diuretic.
Cooking time approx. 20 min
Allergens: L
2 portions to 310,5g. / 166kcal. - (carb:82% / prot:18%)
100g.=53,62kcal. / protein 4,33g. fat:2,25g.
µg. - Ph:8,31 Na:2,83 Ka:26,32 Mg:3,14 Ca:5,9 Fe:0,2 Zn:0,07 Col.:0 Hsr.:6,32

Quantity of ingredients:
Rice variety any 1/2 cup / 60g. (yes)
Water 3 cups / 300g. (yes)
Lemon peel 1 piece / 3g. (yes)
Water 1/2 cup / 0g. (yes)
Carrot 2 pieces / 180g. (yes)
Celery sticks 1/2 piece / 5g. (yes)
Champignon 1/2 cup / 50g. (little)
Cress 2 table spoons / 20g. (yes)
Linseed oil 1 dash / 3g. (yes)

Cooking instructions:
Cook rice according to basic recipe with a piece of lemon peel.
Steam chopped carrots, celery and mushrooms until soft.
Then sprinkle with cress. Then add a dash of high quality cold oil.

9.45 Roasted millet with plum compote

Supports urination, promotes spleen and kidney, strengthens the defense. Good to fight fungi infections.
Cooking time approx. 30 min
4 portions to 218,25g. / 139kcal. - (carb:85% / prot:15%)
100g.=63,8kcal. / protein 3,57g. fat:1,24g.
µg. - Ph:2,99 Na:0,1 Ka:4,37 Mg:1,68 Ca:0,78 Fe:0,09 Zn:0,03 Col.:0 Hsr.:0,93

Quantity of ingredients:
Millet 1 cup / 120g. (yes)
Water 1 1/2 cups / 250g. (yes)
Plum 1 1/2 cups / 250g. (little)
Vanilla pod 1 pinch / 1g. (yes)
Water 5/8 lbs - 8oz / 250g. (yes)
Cinnamon ground 1 pinch / 1g. (little)
Acerola fruit nectar or powder 1/2 teaspoon / 1g. (little)

Cooking instructions:
Roast millet briefly, pour over water, heat till it boils and let stand for 20 min. to swell.
Cook plums with water, vanilla and cinnamon 10 min. then strain. Add acerola and add to the millet.

9.46 Rosemary Potatoes

Reduces Inflammation, improves digestion, regenerates skin, supports urination, lowers cholesterol. Rosemary stimulates digestion, strengthens lung, promotes spleen and kidney, dries out.
Cooking time approx. 30 min
2 portions to 216,5g. / 188kcal. - (carb:76% / prot:24%)
100g.=87,07kcal. / protein 4,21g. fat:5,25g.
µg. - Ph:11,51 Na:0,72 Ka:82,88 Mg:4,72 Ca:1,86 Fe:0,1 Zn:0,07 Col.:0 Hsr.:3,64

Quantity of ingredients:
Potato 6-8 pieces / 420g. (little)
Olive oil 1 table spoon / 10g. (yes)
Rosemary 1 teaspoon / 2g. (yes)

Cooking instructions:
Cut the potatoes into half´s, apply a little olive oil on the cut surface, then salt, sprinkle 2 - 3 rosemary needles on the potatoes.
Place the potatoes on the baking tray and bake them in the preheated oven for approx. 25 minutes to 190°C/374°F.

9.47 Semolina soup with vegetables

Reduces blood pressure, strengthens immune system, prevents cancer, forcing spleen, dissolves stagnation, promotes weight loss. Good to fight immunodeficiency, loss of appetite, flatulence, high blood pressure, depressions, diabetes, diarrhea, rheumatism, heartburn, twelffinger intestinal ulcers.

Cooking time approx. 20 min

Allergens: AGL

3 portions to 237,67g. / 105kcal. - (carb:85% / prot:15%)
100g.=44,32kcal. / protein 2,38g. fat:4,24g.
µg. - Ph:2,88 Na:3,04 Ka:8,54 Mg:9,5 Ca:37,49 Fe:0,11 Zn:0,03 Col.:0 Hsr.:1,7

Quantity of ingredients:

Basic recipe for a vegetable soup (nutritious) 2 cup / 500g. (little)
Wheat semolina 2 table spoons / 20g. (yes)
Lovage 1/2 teaspoon / 2g. (yes)
Basil (fresh) 1/2 teaspoon / 1g. (yes)
Nutmeg 1 pinch / 0,1g. (yes)
Carrot 1/4 lbs - 4oz / 100g. (yes)
Celery root 1/8 lbs - 2oz / 50g. (yes)
Cream, sweet 30% 3 table spoons / 30g. (little)
Parsley 1 table spoon / 10g. (yes)

Cooking instructions:

Roast wheat grits without fat in a pan. Roast the chopped carrots and celery briefly. Add the vegetable soup (Basic recipe for a vegetable soup). Season with lovage, nutmeg and let it 10 min. simmer.
Stir in the cream before serving and garnish with parsley.

9.48 Spicy Tofu Vegetable Pan

Forcing spleen, relieves constipation, detoxifying, reduces inflammation, improves blood circulation, promotes sweating, dissolves stagnation, reduces flatulence, reduces blood pressure, strengthens immune system, prevents cancer, reduces radiation damage.

Cooking time approx. 25 min

Allergens: EN

4 portions to 329,25g. / 241kcal. - (carb:67% / prot:33%)
100g.=73,27kcal. / protein 7,37g. fat:7,32g.
µg. - Ph:3,76 Na:4,32 Ka:9,86 Mg:2,38 Ca:3,32 Fe:0,08 Zn:0,02 Col.:0,01 Hsr.:1,82

Quantity of ingredients:
Sesame oil 2 table spoons / 20g. (little)
Carrot 2 pieces / 100g. (yes)
Fennel 1 piece / 250g. (yes)
Leek 1 piece / 200g. (yes)
Salt 1 pinch / 1g. (little)
Turmeric (yellow root) 1 pinch / 1g. (little)
Lemon juice 1 splash / 1g. (yes)
Soy Tofu 1 package / 120g. (little)
Pepper (ground) 1 pinch / 0,5g. ()
Soy sauce 1 dash / 3g. (little)
Rice (whole grain) 1 cup / 120g. (yes)
Water 6 cups / 500g. (yes)
Salt 1 pinch / 1g. (little)

Cooking instructions:
Heat sesame oil in a hot wok or a hot pan; fry the chopped carrots,
fennel and leek slices; salt, a dash of lemon juice, turmeric, tofu cubes
roast for 1 - 2 minutes.
Add the pepper and cook covered for about 5 minutes; drizzle with soy
sauce.
Place the rice in salted water, heat till it boils and let it simmer over low
heat for about 15 minutes.

9.49 Spring salad

Blood-forming, blood detoxifying, diuretic, good to fight stomach
discomfort, improves digestion, diarrhea, helps to digest fat, supports
urination, reduces blood pressure, detoxifying, reduces inflammation,
diuretic.
Cooking time approx. 10 min
Allergens: AEMNO
4 portions to 214,25g. / 180kcal. - (carb:64% / prot:36%)
100g.=84,13kcal. / protein 7,68g. fat:5,56g.
µg. - Ph:14,38 Na:19,94 Ka:78,76 Mg:7,01 Ca:20,61 Fe:0,72 Zn:0,03 Col.:0 Hsr.:7,87

Quantity of ingredients:
Sorrel 3/8 lbs - 6oz / 150g. (little)
Dandelion (young plants) 1/4 lbs - 4oz / 100g. (yes)
Mung bean sprouting 0,2 lbs / 75g. (little)
Cress 1/4 lbs - 4oz / 100g. (yes)
Chives 1 Bunch / 50g. (yes)
Tomato 2 pieces / 100g. (yes)
Parsley 1 Bunch / 50g. (yes)

Soy sauce 1 dash / 3g. (little)
White bread (wheat bread) 6 slices / 120g. (yes)
Vinegar Aceto Balsamico / 8g. (yes)
Olive oil / 8g. (yes)

Cooking instructions:
Wash all salad's, mix and prepare the sauce as follows:
Mix tahini with mustard and balsamic vinegar, tamari, olive oil, chives
and half of parsley. Pour the sauce over the salad and sprinkle the
remaining parsley just before serving.
Serve with the white bread.

9.50 Thick pea soup

Supports urination, detoxifying, dissolves stagnation, improves blood
circulation, strengthens liver and kidney, strengthens immune system.
Cooking time approx. 2-3 hours
Allergens: AN
3 portions to 255g. / 123kcal. - (carb:47% / prot:53%)
100g.=48,37kcal. / protein 4,36g. fat:7,3g.
µg. - Ph:3,44 Na:0,25 Ka:7,5 Mg:1,22 Ca:1,55 Fe:0,06 Zn:0,04 Col.:0
Hsr.:5,21

Quantity of ingredients:
Peas, green 3/8 lbs - 6oz / 150g. (little)
Water 2 1/4 cups / 550g. (yes)
Sesame oil 1 table spoon / 20g. (little)
Onion white 1/2 piece / 25g. (yes)
Ginger fresh 1/2 teaspoon / 1g. (yes)
Ground 1/2 teaspoon / 1g. (yes)
Oat meal 1 table spoon / 15g. (yes)
Salt 1 pinch / 1g. (little)
Parsley 1 stem / 2g. (yes)

Cooking instructions:
Soak dried peas before cooking. Sauté sesame oil, onion, a little
oatmeal, ginger and cumin in a hot pot; add the peas and simmer for 2-
3 hours; add salt at the end and purée with a blender; garnish with
parsley.

9.51 Vegetable miso soup with tofu

Very powerful, strengthens after febrile illness, reduces blood pressure, strengthens immune system, prevents cancer, reduces radiation damage, improves blood circulation, strengthens liver and kidney, detoxifying, strengthens the muscles, reduces flatulence, forcing spleen.
Cooking time approx. 15 min
Allergens: EN
4 portions to 247,75g. / 107kcal. - (carb:22% / prot:78%)
100g.=43,09kcal. / protein 1,85g. fat:9,4g.
µg. - Ph:3,92 Na:13,88 Ka:10,98 Mg:1,98 Ca:4,08 Fe:0,07 Zn:0,01 Col.:0 Hsr.:1,45

Quantity of ingredients:
Sesame oil 2 table spoons / 35g. (little)
Onion (shallot) 1 piece / 20g. (yes)
Carrot 1 piece / 70g. (yes)
Leek 2 inches / 10g. (yes)
Water 3 cups / 750g. (yes)
Endive salad 2 table spoons / 30g. (yes)
Soy Tofu 2 table spoons / 30g. (little)
Ginger fresh 1/2 teaspoon / 1g. (yes)
Miso 2 table spoons / 15g. (little)

Cooking instructions:
In sesame oil first sauté onions, then carrots and a little leek; Pour in water and simmer gently; add the bean sprouts and endive leaves and leave to stand; Tofu cubes, add a little ginger; at the end stir in a little cooled cooking-water the Miso.

9.52 Vegetable rice

Forcing spleen, dissolves stagnation, promotes weight loss. Good to fight immunodeficiency, loss of appetite, flatulence, high blood pressure, strengthens kidney and bladder. Diuretic, warming the body from the inside, regulates internal organs functions.
Cooking time approx. 30 min
Allergens: L
3 portions to 274,67g. / 304kcal. - (carb:88% / prot:12%)
100g.=110,56kcal. / protein 8,1g. fat:3,4g.
µg. - Ph:11,8 Na:1,92 Ka:15,55 Mg:11,36 Ca:27,38 Fe:0,16 Zn:0,07 Col.:0 Hsr.:5,17

Quantity of ingredients:
Broccoli 1/8 lbs - 2oz / 50g. (little)
Carrot 1/8 lbs - 2oz / 50g. (yes)
Kohlrabi 1/8 lbs - 2oz / 50g. (little)
Cauliflower 1 oz / 30g. (yes)
Peas 1/2 oz / 20g. (little)
Margarine 1 teaspoon / 4g. (yes)
Rice (whole grain) 5/8 oz / 200g. (yes)
Basic recipe for a vegetable soup (nutritious) 7/8 lbs / 400g. (little)
Parsley 1/2 oz / 20g. (yes)
Pepper (ground) 1 pinch / 0,2g. ()

Cooking instructions:
Cut the broccoli, carrots and kohlrabi into small cubes, divide the cauliflower into small florets. Heat the margarine in a pan or saucepan, sauté the vegetables. Then add the rice, top up with the vegetable stock and leave to soak for 15-20 minutes.
In the meantime, finely chop the parsley. After cooking, season the rice with freshly ground pepper and parsley.

9.53 Vegetable semolina soup

Diuretic, harmonizes the stomach and intestines, conducts bowel winds, reduces blood pressure, lowers cholesterol, detoxifying, good to fight loss of appetite, flatulence. Stimulates digestion, reduces pain.
Cooking time approx. 20 min
Allergens: AEGL
3 portions to 459,67g. / 199kcal. - (carb:79% / prot:21%)
100g.=43,22kcal. / protein 6,38g. fat:7,02g.
µg. - Ph:4,26 Na:4,63 Ka:23,27 Mg:6,33 Ca:22,08 Fe:0,09 Zn:0,04 Col.:0,39 Hsr.:2,88

Quantity of ingredients:
Basic recipe for a vegetable soup (nutritious) 2 cup / 500g. (little)
Potato 1 piece / 80g. (little)
Parsnip 1 piece / 180g. (yes)
Carrot 1 piece / 120g. (yes)
Celery root 3/8 lbs - 6oz / 150g. (yes)
Kohlrabi 1/2 piece / 200g. (little)
Beans (green, fresh) 1/4 lbs / 100g. (little)
Wheat semolina 2 table spoons / 24g. (yes)
Lovage 1/2 teaspoon / 2g. (yes)
Butter organic 1 table spoon / 20g. (yes)
Soy sauce 1 teaspoon / 3g. (little)

Cooking instructions:

Worm the prepared vegetable soup; cook the vegetables in the soup softly. Spread some wheatgrass and let it swell. At the end, add lovage-green and a little butter and taste with soy sauce.

9.54 Warming carrot soup

Strengthens and warms, reduces blood pressure, strengthens immune system, prevents cancer, reduces radiation damage, strengthens gastrointestinal function.

Cooking time approx. 30 min

Allergens: HL

3 portions to 274,67g. / 133kcal. - (carb:79% / prot:21%)
100g.=48,54kcal. / protein 2,16g. fat:7,86g.
µg. - Ph:2,86 Na:2,31 Ka:9,18 Mg:8,37 Ca:32,64 Fe:0,13 Zn:0,03 Col.:0 Hsr.:1

Quantity of ingredients:

Carrot 4 pieces / 250g. (yes)
Walnut oil 2 table spoons / 20g. (little)
Onion (shallot) 2 pieces / 40g. (yes)
Anise (Common Fennel) 1/2 teaspoon / 1g. (yes)
Nutmeg 1 pinch / 1g. (yes)
Ginger fresh 1/2 teaspoon / 1g. (yes)
Salt 1 pinch / 1g. (little)
Basic recipe for a vegetable soup (nutritious) 2 cup / 500g. (little)
Parsley 1 table spoon / 10g. (yes)

Cooking instructions:

Heat walnut oil in a hot pot and fry onions; steam the carrots in it; add anise, nutmeg, a little ginger, salt and sauté everything; add water or vegetable- or meat stock; cook everything soft and then puree; fold in parsley at the end.

Recommendation: Suitable for the cold season, especially if you use meat broth as a liquid for infusion.

9.55 Wheat semolina with olives-herb-sauce and salad

Protects the digestive system. Detoxifying, affects anorexia, good to
fight flatulence, inflammatory bowel disease, obesity, gout, stomach
ulcers, stomach cramps, rheumatism, heartburn. Dissolves stagnation,
relieves fatigue.

Cooking time approx. 15 min

Allergens: ACGL

3 portions to 291g. / 245kcal. - (carb:77% / prot:23%)
100g.=84,08kcal. / protein 7,65g. fat:9,46g.
µg. - Ph:4,44 Na:2,51 Ka:6,39 Mg:7,97 Ca:30,53 Fe:0,1 Zn:0,04 Col.:3,02 Hsr.:2,72

Quantity of ingredients:
Cream, sweet 30% 1/8 lbs - 2oz / 40g. (little)
Water 1/3 cup / 65g. (yes)
Wheat semolina 1/4 lbs - 4oz / 100g. (yes)
Chicken egg 1 piece / 60g. (yes)
Pepper (ground) 1 pinch / 0,5g. ()
Lemon peel 1 pinch / 1g. (yes)
Onion white 1 piece / 60g. (yes)
Olive oil 1 teaspoon / 2g. (yes)
Chives 1 table spoon / 7g. (yes)
Basic recipe for a vegetable soup (nutritious) 2 cups / 500g. (little)
Lettuce 2 handful / 30g. (yes)
Olive oil 1 teaspoon / 3g. (yes)
Lemon juice 1 teaspoon / 3g. (yes)
Oregano fresh 1 teaspoon / 2g. (yes)

Cooking instructions:
Mix cream and water and heat till it boils. Stir in the wheat semolina and
cook to a thick porridge and remove from heat. Whisk the egg and stir
in, season with pepper and grated lemon zest. Form with 2 coffee
spoons, dumplings and leave to stir in the slightly boiling vegetable
stock until the dumplings float up.
Chop the onion and roast it in olive oil in a pan. Pour the semolina
dumplings into the pan and sprinkle with finely chopped chives.

Wash salad and cut into thin strips. Season with olive oil, lemon juice
and oregano.

9.56 Zucchini semolina cream soup

Good to fight loss of appetite, reduces blood pressure, promotes weight loss. Good to fight loss of appetite, flatulence, inflammatory bowel disease, rheumatism, heartburn.
Cooking time approx. 25 min
Allergens: AGL
4 portions to 341,75g. / 146kcal. - (carb:78% / prot:22%)
100g.=42,72kcal. / protein 4,02g. fat:7,8g.
µg. - Ph:1,7 Na:0,83 Ka:9,09 Mg:4,88 Ca:18,35 Fe:0,08 Zn:0,02 Col.:0,22 Hsr.:0,82

Quantity of ingredients:
Butter organic 1/2 oz / 20g. (yes)
Wheat semolina 2 table spoons / 20g. (yes)
Parsley 1 Bunch / 100g. (yes)
Basic recipe for a vegetable soup (nutritious) 3 1/2 cups / 800g. (little)
Lovage 1/2 teaspoon / 2g. (yes)
Nutmeg 1 pinch / 0,5g. (yes)
Anise (Common Fennel) 1 pinch / 0,5g. (yes)
Zucchini 7/8 lbs / 400g. (yes)
Ginger fresh 1/2 teaspoon / 1g. (yes)
Crème fraiche cheese 2 table spoons / 20g. (little)
Lemon peel 1/4 piece / 2g. (yes)
Salt 1 pinch / 1g. (little)
Pepper (ground) 1 pinch / 0,5g. ()

Cooking instructions:
Melt the butter in a saucepan, add the semolina and fry briefly while stirring. Add half of the chopped parsley, sauté for a short time, pour vegetable broth according to the basic recipe, season with chopped lovage, nutmeg and anise. Cook the soup without lid lightly for 10 minutes. Add the finely chopped zucchini and the small piece of lemon zest, cook gently for 5 minutes until the zucchini are tender. Remove the lemon peel.
Using the blender, finely puree the soup with the crème fraiche and the remaining parsley

10 Effects of food

10.1 Use ingredients: recommendable

Fresh cheese from soya
Noodles (wheat) with egg
Noodles (wheat, lasagne) with egg
Noodles (wheat, spaghetti) with egg
Noodles (whole grain) with egg

10.2 Use ingredients: yes

Adzuki beans
Agar agar (kelp)
Agave nectar
Angelica root
Anise (Common Fennel)
Arrowroot
Asparagus (green or white)
Aubergine
Avocado
Balm
Bamboo shoots
Banchatee (green tea)
barberry
Barley
Barley flour
Barley grass powder
Barley grouts
Barley malt
Barley not peeled
Basil
Basil (fresh)
Batavia
Bay leaf
Bearberry leaf
Bitter Herb liqueur
Bitter Lemon
Bitter melon
Bitter orange peel
Black caraway
Blackberry leaves
Blue mallow tee
Borage
Borage oil
Boxhorn clover seeds
Bread roll
Bread with carob kernel flour
Breadcrumbs (wheat bread, bread roll)
Buckbean
Buckwheat
Buckwheat (roasted) Kasha
Buckwheat whole grain
Bulgur (cereals)
Burdock root tea

Butter (half fat)
Butter organic
Capers in olive oil
Carob flour, St. john's bread
Carrot
Carrot (Early Carrot)
Carrot juice without sugar
Cauliflower
Celery root
Celery sticks
Cereal coffee
Chamomile
Chervil
Chervil dried
Chicken egg
Chicken egg white
Chicken meat
Chicken yolk
Chicory
Chili (pod or ground)
Chives
Chlorella (fresh water)
Chrysanthemum blossom tea
Cinnamon sticks
Clarified butter
Clove
Coconut flakes
Coconut grated
Coconut meat
Coconut milk
Cooking oil
Coriander
Coriander (fresh)
Corn
Corn (fast polenta)
Corn (roasted)
Corn flour
Corn germ oil
Corn Grease (Polenta)
Corn silk tea
Corn starch
Couscous
Cream sour 10%

Creamer
Cress
Crispbread
Cucumber
Cucumber (spicy cucumber)
Cumin (Caraway seed)
Curcuma
Curry
Curry paste red
Daisy
Dandelion (young plants)
Dandelion juice
Dandelionroots tea
Dashi
Dates dried
Dates red
Dill
Dyer's broom herb
Elderberry blossom tee
Endive salad
Evening primrose oil
Fennel
Fennel seeds ground
Fennel tea
Fenugreek (Trigonella foenum-graecum)
Flounder
Flower pollen
Fox nut, gorgon nut, makhana
Fresh cheese with herbs
Fructose (glucose)
Garam Masala powder
Garlic
Gelee Royal
Gentian root
Ginger fresh
Ginger oil
Ginger powder
Ginseng root
Gourd
Grapefruit (Pomelo)
Grapefruit dried peel
Grapefruit juice
Grapes red
Grapes white
Grapeseed oil
Green tea
Ground
Ground caraway
Hawthorn
Herbal tea mix
Herbs bitter
Herbs of Provence
Herbs various

Herbs wild
Hibiscus
Hibiscus tea
Hokkaido pumpkin
Honey
Horehound leaves
Hyssop
Iceberg lettuce
Jasmine blossoms tee
Juniper berry
King Solomon's-seal
Kukicha tea
Kumquats
Lamb's lettuce
Lavender blossoms
Leaf salads (bitter)
Leek
Lemon
Lemon Balm (dried)
Lemon Balm (fresh)
Lemon juice
Lemon peel
Lemongrass
Lettuce
Lime
Lime blossom tea
Linseed oil
Liver smoothing tea
Lotus roots
Lotus seeds
Lovage
Lovage seeds
Luo Han Guo fruit
Lye roll
Mallow (Malva sylvestris) blossom tea
Malt
Maple syrup
Margarine
Margarine (diet)
Marjoram
Millet
Millet flakes
Mulled Wine Spice
Multi-grain bread (gray bread)
Nasturtium (nose-twister or nose-tweaker)
Nettles
Nori, purple seaweed, red algae
Nutmeg
Oat
Oat flakes (whole grain)
Oat flakes roasted
Oat flour
Oat fusion (baby food)

Oat meal
Olive oil
Olives
Olives green
Onion (shallot)
Onion (spring onion)
Onion read
Onion white
Oregano dried
Oregano fresh
Palm oil
Parsley
Parsley root
Parsnip
Passion blossoms tea
Pearl barley
Pearl barley
Pepper Cayenne
Pepper white (ground)
Peppercorns
Peppermint
Peppermint tea
Pepperoni
Pepperoni, red, pitted, halved
Pepperoni, yellow, pitted, halved
Peppers
Peppers (rose peppers)
Peppers (sweet)
Pickle
Psyllium seed
Pudding powder vanilla
Puff pastry
Pumpkin
Pumpkin seed oil
Radicchio
Radish
Radish (white, green, purple-red)
Radish black
Radish horseradish
Radish leaves
Rapeseed oil
Raspberry leaf tea
Red beet
Red berry (without sugar)
Ribworttea
Rice (fragrance)
Rice (Gaoliang / Sorghum)
Rice (whole grain)
Rice Basmati
Rice black
Rice flour
Rice long grain rice
Rice malt
Rice mash

Rice noodles
Rice red
Rice round grain
Rice starch
Rice sticky
Rice sweet
Rice variety any
Rice wild (nature rice)
Rose blossom tea
Rose leaf tea
Rosemary
Rusk
Rye
Rye flour
Safflower (Dyer's thistle / Hong Hua)
Sage
Sago (cereals)
Salsify
Sourdough
Spelled flakes
Spelled grain
Spelled semolina
Spurdog (spiny dogfish, Schillerlocken)
St. Benedict's thistle, blessed thistle,
holy thistle, spotted thistle
Strawberry jam
Sugar - icing sugar
Sugar brown
Sugar candy white
Sugar cane sugar
Sugar fructose - fruit sugar
Sugar glucose - grapes sugar
Sugar Milk Sugar
Sugar molasses
Sugar palm sugar
Sugar substitute (sweetener)
Sugar white
Tarragon (Estragon)
Tea mixture uric acid lowering
Thistle oil
Thyme
Thyme dried
Tomato
Tomato puree
Valerian
Vanilla
Vanilla pod
Vanilla powder
Vanilla sugar natural
Vinegar (Apple vinegar)
Vinegar (Red wine vinegar)
Vinegar Aceto Balsamico
Vinegar Aceto Balsamico white
Water

Water hot
Watermelon
Wax gourd
Wheat
Wheat bulgur
Wheat flakes
Wheat flatbread/pita bread
Wheat flour
Wheat germ oil
Wheat semolina
Wheat semolina for children
Wheatgrass juice
Wheatgrass powder
White bread (baguette)
White bread (pretzel sticks)
White bread (roll)

White bread (wheat bread)
White breadcrumbs
White dumpling bread (wheat bread cut into chunks)
Wild garlic (garlic spinach)
Wild herbs
Wild strawberries
Wormwood herb
Yam root, yam root tuber
Yarrow
Yarrow tea
Yoghurt vanilla
Yogi tea
Yogurt (natural, 1.5% fat)
Yogurt (natural, 3.5% fat)
Zucchini

10.3 Use ingredients: little

Acerola fruit nectar or powder
Agrimony
Aloe juice
Amaranth
Amaranth Pops
Anchovy / Sardine
Apple (sour)
Apple (sweet)
Apple puree
Apricot
Apricot jam
Apricots
Artichoke
Baking powder
Basic recipe for a beef soup
Basic recipe for a beef soup (warming)
Basic recipe for a chicken soup (warming)
Basic recipe for a duck soup
Basic recipe for a fish soup
Basic recipe for a rice soup (Congee)
Basic recipe for a vegetable soup (nutritious)
Bean oil
Beans (green, fresh)
Beef bone marrow
Beef fillet
Beef heart
Beef heart (calf)
Beef kidney
Beef liver
Beef lungs (calf)
Beef meat
Beef meat (calf)

Beef meatbones
Beef Oxtail pieces
Beef soup meat
Beef stomach
Berries of the season
Bitter liqueur
Black beans
Black fungus mushroom
Black tea
Blackberry dried (unripe fruit)
Blackberry jam
Blackberry´s
Black-eyed peas
Blackthorn (Sloe)
Blueberry
Blueberry dried
Blueberry jam
Bocksdorn fruits (Fructus Lycii, Goji, goji berry dried
Brazil nuts
Brie cheese
Broad beans (thick beans)
Broccoli
Brown ale
Brussels sprouts
Bush beans
Butter beans white
Buttermilk
Calamari
Camembert
Campari
Cantaloupe
Carambola (Star fruit)
Cardamom

Carp
Cashews
Caviar
Champignon
Channa-Dal
Chenpi (chinese tangerine bowl)
Cherry
Cherry (sour)
Cherry compote
Chestnuts
Chicken Blood
Chicken heart
Chicken liver
Chicken stomach
Chickpeas
Chickweed
Chinese cabbage
Chinese pearl barley
Cinnamon ground
Clementine
Clementines
Cocoa
Coconut fat
Cod
Codfish
Coffee
Coix (seeds) YiYi Ren
Compote (fruits of the season)
Cottage cheese
Cow's milk (1.5% fat)
Cow's milk (whole milk 3.5% fat)
Crab
Cranberries
Cranberry
Cranberry
Cranberry jam
Cranberry juice
Cream (30% fat)
Cream sour 20%
Cream sour 30%
Cream, sweet 30%
Créme fraiche cheese
Crucian
Curd cheese 20%
Curd cheese 40%
Currant (black)
Currant (red)
Currant (white)
Currant jam (black)
Currant jam (red)
Deer meat
Deer meat
Deer's Bones
Deer's kidneys

Duck (heart)
Duck (slaughtered)
Ducks egg
Dulse (seaweed)
Edam cheese
Eel
Eel smoked
Elderberries
Fernet Branca (herbal bitter liqueur)
Feta cheese
Feta cheese
Fig
Fish innards
Fish pieces mixed (fresh water)
Fish remains
Fish sauce
French beans
Fresh cheese
Freshwater crab
Freshwater fish
Gail plum
Galangal
Gelatin white
Ginkgo fruit
Ginseng liqueur
Goat
Goat and sheep's blood
Goat and sheep's brain
Goat and sheep's liver
Goat and sheep's milk
Goat and sheep's stomach
Goat cheese
Goose
Goose blood
Goose egg
Goose fat
Goose parts
Gooseberry
Gorgonzola
Gouda cheese
Grape juice red
Grape juice white
Grass carp
Green spelt
Greengage
Guava
Halibut (Flatfish)
Herring
Hijiki
Honey wine (Met)
Hop
Horse meat
Jellyfish
Kaki plum

Kalmus	Mussels
Kefir	Mustard
Kidney beans (red)	Mustard Dijon
Kiwi	Mustard medium hot
Kohlrabi	Mustard seeds
Kombu seaweed (Saccharina japonica)	Mustard sweet
Ladyfingers	Mutton
Lamb bones	Mutton
Lamb kidneys	Nectarine
Lamb liver	Oat milk
Lamb meat	Octopus
Lamb shoulder	Octopus
Lamb's lettuce	Okra
Lentils	Orange
Lentils black	Orange blossom
Lentils red	Orange dried peel
Lentils yellow	Orange grated peel
Licorice root tea	Orange jam
Lima beans	Orange peel
Linseed	Oyster shell powder
Linseed (crushed)	Papaya
Lobster	Passion fruit
Longane	Peaches
Loquate / Japanese medlar	Peaches (canned)
Lychee	Peanut (roasted)
Lychee in Preserved	Peanut butter
Lychee liqueur	Peanut oil
Mackerel	Peanuts
Mango	Pear
Mango juice	Peas
Manioc flour	Peas, green
Mare's milk	Pepper powder (hot)
Martini	Peppers powder
Mayonnaise 50%	Perch
Mayonnaise 80%	Pheasant
Mediterranean fish (cod, plaice,	Pig blood
haddock, sea eel, mackerel)	Pigeon
Medlar	Pigeon egg
Mineral water	Pimento
Mirabelle plum	Pine nuts
Miso	Pineapple
Miso black (fermented)	Pineapple juice without sugar
Miso paste (soy bean paste)	Pinto beans speckled
Mixed Pickles	Plaice
Mold cheese	Plum
Morel (black, dried)	Plums
Morel, dried	Pomegranate
Mozzarella	Pork Bacon
Mu Erh Mushroom	Pork brain
Muesli	Pork fat (lard)
Mulberry fruit	Pork ham
Mullet	Pork ham cooked
Mung bean	Pork ham smoked
Mung bean sprouting	Pork heart

Pork kidneys
Pork knuckle
Pork Lard
Pork liver
Pork lung
Pork marrow bones
Pork meat
Pork skin
Pork stomach
Pork/beef sausage (smoked)
Pork's intestine
Potato
Potato (mealy)
Potato flour
Prickly pear
Prosecco
Pumpernickel (dark bread)
Pumpkin seeds
Quail
Quail egg
Quince
Quinoa
Rabbit
Rabbit (wild)
Rabbit liver
Rabbit meat
Raspberry
Raspberry dried (immature)
Raspberry jam
Red cabbage
Reishi mushroom
Rhubarb
Romaine lettuce / lettuce salad
Rose hip
Rose hip tea
Rosefish
Rum
Rye wholemeal bread
Saffron
Sake
Salmon
Salt
Salt (herbal)
Sauerkraut (cutted cabbage fermented)
Savory
Savoy cabbage / kale
Sea buckthorn
Sea cucumber
Seacrab
Sesame oil
Sesame oil roasted
Shark
Sheep's milk
Sheep's milk yoghurt

Sherry (whine)
Shrimp
Shrimps
Skim milk powder
Slug
Sorrel
Sour cherries
Sour cream 15% fat
Sour milk
Sour milk cheese 20%
Soy flour
Soy noodles
Soy sauce
Soy Tofu
Soy Tofu smoked
Soya Cuisine (soy cream)
Soybean milk
Soybean oil
Soybeans
Soybeans, black
Soybeans, blacks, fermented
Soybeans, yellow
Spelled (Dark) bread
Spelled wholemeal flour
Spiny lobsters
Spirit
Star anise
Stevia (candyleaf, sweetleaf)
Strawberries
Strawberry Juice
Sunflower oil
Sweet potato
Tabasco
Tangerine
Toast bread (whole grain)
Tomato dried
Tomato juice
Tomato paste
Tonic Water
Trout
Truffle
Tsampa (roasted barley flour)
Tuna
Turkey breast meat
Turkey ham
Turmeric (yellow root)
Turnip
Turnips
Umeboshi paste
Umeboshi plums (Japanese apricots)
Vegetable juice
Wakame
Walnut oil
Wheat beer

Wheat bran
Wheat flour whole grain
Wheat/Rye/Gray-black bread with yeast
Whey
White beans
White cabbage
White wine

Whitefish
Whole grain bread
Wholemeal flour
Wild boar meat
Wormwood
Yeast
Yew nut

10.4 Do not use contra-acting foods

Almond
Almond marzipan
Almond milk
Almond puree
Apple juice (natural cloudy)
Apricot dried
Apricot nectar
Apricots juice
Banana
Banana (cooking banana)
Beer (alcohol-free)
Beer (alcohol-reduced)
Beer (Pils)
Beer (Top-fermented German dark beer)
Berry juice
Blueberry juice
Boletus mushroom
Chanterelle
Chard
Cherry juice
Chocolate
Chocolate (Diabetic)
Cola drink
Cola drink (low calorie)
Currant juice (black)
Currants (black)
Currants (red)
Emmental cheese

Fig dried
Fruit mix juice
Fruit tea
Hazelnuts
Orange juice
Oyster mushroom
Oysters
Parmesan
Pear juice
Pineapple (from a can)
Pistachios
Plum dried
Poppy
Pork sausage (Bratwurst) Processed cheese 12%
processed cheese 30%
Raisins
Red wine
Sesame paste (Tahini)
Sesame, black
Sesame, white
Shiitake, dried
Spinach
Sunflower seeds
Supplementary nutrition
Trout (smoked)
Walnuts
Walnuts roasted

11 Complementary

11.1 Bath for purification

preparation: Healing bath
A bath for purification (base bath), stimulates the natural regeneration of the skin and thus supports the excretion of acids and metabolic waste. The longer you bathe, the more effective the bath is.
Purification bath additive available at the pharmacy or drugstore.

11.2 Birch leaves

Folium Betulae
preparation: Healing tea (infusion)
This tea is diuretic and helps against kidney ailments, gout and cleans the blood, also helps with bacterial and inflammatory urinary tract diseases, kidney grief and rheumatic complaints.
Pour 2 tablespoons of crushed birch leaves into 250 ml of boiling water, let stand for 10 minutes. Then sieve.
Drink one cup of it a day.

11.3 Cress

Herba Nasturtii
preparation: Cooking addition
Diuretic, forces urination.

12 Basics of Nutrition

The basic principles of nutrition described herein are general recommendations. They are not aimed at a specific form of therapy. Recommendations concerning a therapy have priority.

12.1 Nutrition

Regular meals in a relaxed atmosphere. A warm breakfast is considered a good start into the day.
The main meals ought to be taken for lunch – supper in the early evening. Pay attention to feeling hungry or sated: don't eat too much nor remain hungry is the rule
Prepare the meals freshly from natural, regional products. Frozen, heat-conserved, industrially prepared or foodstuffs cooked in the microwave oven are rejected.
Choice of foodstuffs according to the season: more cooling food in summer, more warming food in winter.
Eat cooked food at least twice a day. Food and drinks ought to be lukewarm, never ice-cold or hot.
Raw vegetables, briefly cooked vegetables, freshly squeezed juices and mineral water are not recommended. Milk and dairy products are only included in the diet if they don't cause problems.
Don't use therapeutic recipes over a longer period without consulting your doctor or therapist.

Varied food
Enjoy the diversity of foodstuffs. Characteristics of a balanced nutrition are variety, suitable combination and a balanced quantity of rich and low energy foodstuffs (on one hand avoiding undersupply with essential nutrients and on the other hand to take to many undesirable substances).

A lot of Cereal Products - and Potatoes
Bread, pasta, rice, cereal flakes (best wholemeal) as well as potatoes contain almost no fat, but many vitamins, mineral nutrients, trace elements, roughage and secondary plant substances. These foodstuffs ought to be taken with low-fat side dishes.

Vegetables and Fruit – „Take Five" every day ...
5 portions of vegetables and fruit a day, as fresh as possible, briefly cooked, or maybe one portion as a juice – ideal as a side dish to every meal as well as snack between meals: Thus a lot of vitamins, mineral nutrients as well as roughage and secondary plant substances

Daily milk and dairy products
Milk and Dairy Products every Day, once or twice per Week Fish; meat, sausages as well as eggs moderately. These foodstuffs contain valuable nutrients like calcium in the milk, iodine selenium and omega-3 fat acids in saltwater fish. Meat is favorable due to its high content of disposable iron and the vitamins B1, B6 and B12. Quantities of 300 – 600 g meat and sausage per week are sufficient. Prefer low-fat products, especially in meat- and dairy products.

Low-fat and fatty Foodstuffs
Fat supplies us with essential fat acids and fatty foodstuffs contain also fat-soluble vitamins. Fat is high in energy; therefore much fat in the food may cause overweight, possibly also cancer. Too many saturated fat acids may further a tendency for cardio-vascular diseases in the long term. Prefer vegetable oils and fats (e.g. rapeseed-, olive-, soya-oils and solid fats produced therefrom). Beware of invisible fat in meat- and dairy products, pastry and sweets as well as in fast-food and convenience foods. 70 – 90 g fat per day is sufficient.

Moderately Sugar and Salt
Take sugar and foods/drinks containing various kinds of sugar (e.g. glucose syrup) only occasionally. Use herbs and spices as well as a little salt creatively. Prefer salt containing iodine.

Plenty of Liquids
Water is absolutely essential. Drink 1-2 l liquids every day. Prefer water (with or without gas) and other low-calorie drinks. Alcoholic drinks should not be taken.

Tasty Dishes, carefully cooked
Cook the meals with as low temperatures and as short as possible, using little water and fat – this preserves the original taste, keeps the nutrients intact and prevents the production of harmful compounds.

Take time and enjoy the food
Take your Time and enjoy your Food
Eating consciously helps to eat right. The eye enjoys food, too. It's fun, invites to enjoy varied dishes and stimulates the feeling of satiety.

Watch your Weight and stay in Motion
A balanced diet and a lot of exercise and sport (30 – 60 min/day) are a healthy combination. The right weight furthers well-being and health. Thermals, directional effectiveness, digestive power

There are various criteria for judging the effectiveness of herbs and foodstuffs.

The use of certain herbs and ingredients is based on observations of the effects on the body which these foodstuffs, herbs and spices show after having eaten them. The medical science has developed following system: Every ingredient or herb has a directional effectiveness. Furthermore, there are herbs which have a special effect on certain organs.

The basic condition for a healthy metabolism is to obtain sufficient energy from food and that the digestive process doesn't use too much energy. An easily digestible meal makes content and sated, doesn't cause flatulence and fatigue after the meal. The perfect spices increase the healthiness of our meals. Very often, just small doses of herbs and spices will suffice. They are not used to make us sated, but to help our digestive organs to digest the food.

12.2 Recipes

The recipes list the ingredients to be used and the cooking instructions show how the dish is prepared. The list of ingredients shows the concerned quantities as well as the relevance for the therapy. If you find „less than mentioned", try to comply or find an alternative from the „list of recommended foodstuffs". Mostly it shall result just in a small change of taste when you simply avoid this ingredient.

Mild cooking methods: boiling, stewing, poaching, steaming
Strong cooking methods: barbecuing, roasting, frying, smoking
Balanced cooking methods: deep-frying, baking brick
Deep-freezing and warming in the microwave oven should be avoided (denaturalization).

12.3 Foodstuffs

Foodstuffs have an effect on body and soul like medicinal herbs, only a very much milder one. Dietary advice is mainly based on regional foodstuffs. The knowledge about the effects of each foodstuff and the knowledge, when which foodstuff shall be used, is based on the orthodox school of medicine. Use ecologic-organic products, if possible. As everything should be cooked for a long time due to a better digestability and very rarely eaten raw, the food agrees with everyone.

The classification of the foodstuffs according to their effect on the body is the basis in order to achieve a harmonious status of health.

Dietary advisors do not recommend certain foodstuffs for everyone. The individual diet is tailor-made for the individual constitution.

Buy only fresh and ripe fruit and vegetables. You ought to leave unripe fruit and vegetables and such with brown spots and wilted leaves behind in the market. In this case take deep-frozen goods (never ready-to-serve dishes!). Fruit and vegetables are deep-frozen immediately after harvesting and often contain more vitamins and minerals than the goods from the vegetable shelf. Whereas conserved or tinned goods contain very much less biological substances. Also, salt, sugar and others are mostly added to the latter. Never leave the foodstuffs in the water after washing them to avoid that many vital substances get drowned. Clean salads, fruit and vegetables immediately before serving.

Please make sure of the hygienic processing of foodstuffs. Clean your salads, fruit and vegetables carefully. When cooking with meat, prepare all ingredients first and then process the meat products. Clean the worktop and tools very carefully. Wooden surfaces ought to be treated with a mild disinfectant regularly in order to reduce germination.

Store fruit and vegetables separately, if possible. Harvested fruit and vegetables are still alive and emit e.g. ethylene gas, which makes other products ripen and age faster. Keep meat and fish in the closed packaging or store them in the fridge in closed containers.

12.4 Herbs

There are some basic rules for storing medicinal herbs. On principle, herbs must be protected from direct sunlight, humidity and heat.

Containers for the storage of herbs may be glasses, ceramic jars and even plastic containers. However, plastic is a rather unsuitable material and should only be a short-term solution. In case of glass containers, use a dark material.

Medicinal herbs cannot be kept for any long period. The shelf life of herbs is limited. However, it can be prolonged with suitable storage. The place should be dark, rather cool and absolutely dry. A wooden medicine cabinet, placed not directly next to a source of heat, would be ideal. Never buy large quantities of herbs so as not to have to throw them away. Label the container with the name of the herb and the date of harvesting or processing.

13 Other dietic-books

The following syndromes of dietetics, TCM or for a therapy supplement for cancer are available.

Dietetics

E001. Nutrition of the infant - baby food
E002. Nutrition during lactation
E003. Nutrition in old age
E004. Nutrition of children and adolescents
E005. Nutrition of athletes
E006. Light weight
E007. Pregnancy
E008. Full food

Protein and electrolyte - kidneys
E009. (hemodialysis) dialysis treatment
E010. Acute renal failure
E011. Chronic renal insufficiency
E012. Nephrotic syndrome
E013. Kidney stones (nephrolithiasis)

Gastrointestinal tract - pancreas
E014. Acute pancreatitis (inflammation of the pancreas)
E015. Chronic pancreatitis (inflammation of the pancreas)

Gastrointestinal tract - small intestine and large intestine
E016. Acute obstipation (constipation)
E017. Chronic obstipation (constipation)
E018. Colon irritabile
E019. Diverticulitis
E020. Acquired lactose intolerance (lactose malabsorption)
E021. Fructose malabsorption
E022. Glutensensitive enteropathy (celiac disease)
E023. Colectomy
E024. Short Bowel Syndrome

Gastrointestinal tract - liver, gallbladder, bile ducts
E025. Acute and chronic hepatitis (inflammation of the liver)
E026. Cholelithiasis (bile stones)
E027. fatty liver
E028. cirrhosis

Gastrointestinal tract - Stomach and duodenal intestine
E029. Acute gastritis
E030. Chronic gastritis
E031. Stomach bleeding
E032. Ulcus ventriculi and duodenal ulcer
E033. Condition after gastric surgery

Gastrointestinal tract - oral cavity and esophagus
E034. Stomatitis
E035. Esophageal carcinoma (esophageal cancer)
E036. Refluosophagitis (heartburn)

Special diseases
E037. Phenylketonuria (PKU)
E038. Rheumatic joint diseases

Metabolism
E039. Obesity (overweight)
E040. Diabetes mellitus
E041. Eating disorders (underweight)

Fat metabolism
E042. Hypercholesterolaemia (increased cholesterol level)
E043. Hepatic Encephalopathy

Heart and circulation
E044. Arteriosclerosis (arterial calcification)
E045. Heart insufficiency
E046. Hypertension
E047. Hyperuricaemia and gout

Changed nutrient requirements
E048. In case of fever
E049. For malignant diseases
E050. After burns
E051. Radiation and chemotherapy

CANCER
E100. Pancreatic cancer
E101. Bladder cancer
E102. Blood cancer (leukemia)
E103. Breast cancer
E104. Colorectal cancer
E105. Gastric cancer
E106. Kidney cancer
E107. Esophageal cancer

TCM
E200. Bladder - moisture heat in the bladder
E201. Bladder - moisture and cold in the bladder
E202. Bladder - emptiness and cold in the bladder
E203. Large intestine - external cold affects the large intestine
E204. Large intestine - moisture heat in the large intestine
E205. Large intestine - heat blocks the intestine II acute
E206. Large intestine - dryness of the colon
E207. Large intestine - Yang deficiency (cold)
E208. Heart - Blood insufficiency
E209. Heart - Blood stagnation
E210. Heart - Fire
E211. Heart - Hot mucus clogs the heart pores

E212. Heart - Cold mucus clogs the heart pores
E213. Heart - Qi deficiency
E214. Heart - Yang deficiency
E215. Heart - Yin deficiency
E216. Liver - Ascending Liver Yang
E217. Liver - Blood deficiency
E218. Liver - Blood stagnation
E219. Liver - Moisture heat in liver and gall bladder
E220. Liver - Fire
E221. Liver - Gall bladder Qi-Empty
E222. Liver - Cold in the liver meridian
E223. Liver - Qi stagnation
E224. Liver - Wind
E225. Liver - Wind with ascending liver Yang
E226. Liver - Wind with blood anemic
E227. Liver - Wind with extreme heat
E228. Lung - Qi deficiency
E229. Lung - Mucus-moisture in the lungs
E230. Lung - Mucus-heat in the lungs
E231. Lung - Mucus-cold in the lungs
E232. Lung - Dryness of the lungs
E233. Lung - Wind-heat attacks the lungs
E234. Lung - Wind-cold affects the lungs
E235. Lung - Yin deficiency
E236. Stomach - Bloodstagnation
E237. Stomach - Fire
E238. Stomach - Cold with liquid
E239. Stomach - Nutrition stagnation
E240. Stomach - Qi deficiency
E241. Stomach - Rebellious Qi
E242. Stomach - Yin Emptiness
E243. Spleen - Heat and moisture attack the spleen
E244. Spleen - Coldness and moisture affects the spleen
E245. Spleen - Qi deficiency
E246. Spleen - Qi deficiency + Declining spleen Qi
E247. Spleen - Qi deficiency + spleen does not control the blood
E248. Spleen - Yang deficiency
E249. Kidney - Heart and kidney no longer communicate
E250. Kidney - Jing deficiency
E251. Kidney - Kidneys cannot receive the Qi
E252. Kidney - Qi is not stable
E253. Kidney - Yang deficiency
E254. Kidney - Yin deficiency

For further information visit di-book.com.

14 EBNS - Software for nutritional counseling

The main task of the database is to create personalized nutritional advice for each patient individually. The database was developed for Dietetics and Traditional Chinese Medicine.

The Database supports training and advices in the daily work routine.

The computer program provides lists of recipes, ingredients and herbs, which are given to the client. individually adjustable according to patient's request from whole food to vegetarians (lacto, ovo, ...). For every register there is an information sheet which can be given to the client. All texts can be individually designed.

The syndromes can be combined and result in an intersection of the recommended recipes and ingredients. The automated diagnosis for the TCM enables you to check your experience during the training as well as to confirm your diagnosis in the working day. You select several predefined symptoms and have the program automatically display the relevant syndromes.

How to work with the database:
Select the patient / client, select one or more of the syndromes you diagnosed and print the folder.

You can change all values, create new symptoms or syndromes, develop recipes, change or adapt ingredients and herbs to your findings. In simple client management, all relevant data about the person is stored. You get an overview of the past diagnoses and the development of the course of the disease.

As a consultant you save a lot of time when you print out the recipe, food and herbal lists for the recognized syndromes and give them to the clients. You can use this time for a personal conversation. With the database, dieticians and nutritionists can view the nutrients and trace elements for each recipe and develop recipes for syndromes even with suggested ingredients.

All recipe and grocery lists can also be ordered from me as a combination of several diseases. I wish all readers good luck, health and happiness in life.
More information can be found at www.ebns.at.
Volunteer: www.krebsinfo.at
Josef Miligui